THE UK
TOWER VORTX
DUAL BASKET
AIR FRYER COOKBOOK
FOR BEGINNERS

Easy, Flavorful and Healthy Recipes for Your
Smart Tower Dual Zone to Air Fry, Grill, Roast and
Bake Everyday, with Colour Pictures

Diane Jackson

Table of Contents

INTRODUCTION

Are you tired of juggling between multiple batches while using your single-basket air fryer, wishing for more room and efficiency in your cooking process? If so, you are not alone. I have been there, trying to whip up meals for my family and friends, only to find myself waiting for one batch to finish before starting the next. That's when I discovered the Tower Vortx Duo Basket Air Fryer, a game-changer in my kitchen. Its dual-basket design offers the solution I had been searching for, providing ample space and versatility to cook multiple dishes simultaneously.

In fact, my experience with the Tower Vortx Duo Basket Air Fryer has been so transformative that I decided to create this cookbook. Inside, you will find a collection of mouthwatering recipes specially crafted for this remarkable appliance. From crispy starters and succulent mains to delectable desserts, these recipes are designed to take full advantage of the extra cooking space and convenience offered by the Tower Vortx Duo Basket Air Fryer. Get ready to unlock a world of culinary possibilities and enjoy hassle-free, delicious meals that will impress your loved ones, all thanks to the Tower Vortx Dual Basket Cookbook.

Chapter 1: The Basics of Tower Vortx Duo Basket Air Fryer

The Tower Vortx Duo Basket Air Fryer is a versatile kitchen appliance that stands out for its impressive features. With a generous 9-liter capacity and dual-basket technology, it allows you to cook large meals or multiple dishes simultaneously. The innovative Smart Finish function ensures that different foods with varying cooking times finish at the same time, eliminating the hassle of coordinating meal prep. Powered by a robust 2600W heating element, it quickly reaches and maintains cooking temperatures, while its focus on healthy cooking means you can enjoy delicious, crispy results with minimal to no oil. The sleek black design adds a touch of modernity to your kitchen, making it a practical and stylish addition to your worktop.

Control Panel of the Tower Vortx Duo Basket Air Fryer

- **Basket 1 / Basket 2 Key:** This key allows you to select which basket you want to use, making it easy to cook different dishes simultaneously or choose the most suitable basket for your meal size.

- **Temperature + Key:** Use this key to increase the cooking temperature in increments of 10°C. Precise temperature control ensures your dishes are cooked to perfection.

- **Temperature Indicator:** The LED screen displays the selected cooking temperature, providing real-time feedback on your cooking settings.

- **Temperature – Key:** To lower the cooking temperature, use this key in 10°C increments. Adjusting the temperature allows you to fine-tune your cooking process.

- **LED Screen:** The LED screen provides clear and easy-to-read information about the selected settings, including temperature and time, helping you monitor your cooking progress.

- **Time + Key:** Increase the cooking time in 1-minute intervals using this key. Adjusting the time ensures that your food is cooked for the precise duration you desire.

- **Time Indicator:** This indicator on the LED screen displays the selected cooking time, keeping you informed about the remaining cooking duration.

- **Time – Key:** To decrease the cooking time, use this key in 1-minute increments. Accurate timing is essential for achieving the perfect results.

- **Pre-Heat Key:** The Pre-Heat function allows you to heat the appliance to a specific temperature for a set duration before cooking. Pre-heating is useful for achieving a chargrill effect or extra crispness in your dishes.

- **Start/Pause Key:** Initiate the cooking process by pressing this key, and pause it if necessary. The Start/Pause function provides flexibility during cooking, letting you check on your food or make adjustments as needed.

- **Chips Pre-Set Key:** This pre-set function is optimized for cooking crispy and delicious chips. It simplifies the cooking process by using predefined settings for excellent results.

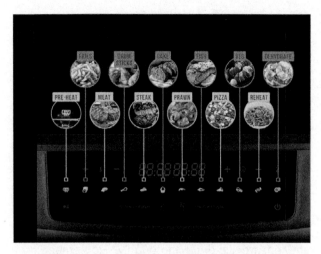

- **Meat Pre-Set Key:** Select this pre-set for cooking various meats, ensuring they are cooked to perfection with the appropriate settings.

- **Drumsticks Pre-Set Key:** Ideal for cooking drumsticks, this pre-set offers tailored settings to achieve crispy, flavourful results.

- **Steak Pre-Set Key:** The Steak pre-set function ensures your steaks are cooked to your desired level of doneness, providing a restaurant-quality experience.

- **Cake Pre-Set Key:** Use this pre-set for baking cakes, tarts, or pies. It simplifies the baking process and ensures your desserts turn out moist and delicious.

- **Smart Finish Key:** The Smart Finish function is a standout feature that coordinates cooking times and temperatures for different foods, ensuring they finish cooking simultaneously.

- **Match Cook Key:** When cooking the same food in both baskets, the Match Cook function ensures consistent cooking by synchronizing settings between the two baskets.

- **Prawn Pre-Set Key:** Tailored for prawn dishes, this pre-set guarantees that your prawns are cooked to perfection with ease.

- **Fish Pre-Set Key:** The Fish pre-set function simplifies cooking fish, maintaining its moisture and flavour for delectable results.

- **Pizza Pre-Set Key:** Ideal for making crispy and perfectly cooked pizzas, this pre-set takes the guesswork out of the cooking process.

- **Vegetables Pre-Set Key:** Use this pre-set to prepare a variety of vegetables with the optimal settings for achieving a great texture and taste.

- **Re-Heat Pre-Set Key:** The Re-Heat pre-set function is designed for efficiently reheating leftovers, ensuring they are warmed through evenly.

- **Power On/Off Button:** This button powers the appliance on and off, allowing you to start or stop the cooking process.

- **Dehydrate Pre-Set Key:** The Dehydrate pre-set function is ideal for making homemade dried fruits, jerky, or snacks, offering precise settings for dehydrating your ingredients.

With these extensive control panel features, the Tower Vortx Duo Basket Air Fryer gives you the flexibility and precision needed to prepare a wide range of dishes with ease, ensuring consistent and delicious results every time you cook.

Benefits of Tower Vortx Duo Basket Air Fryer

The Tower Vortx Duo Basket Air Fryer offers a range of benefits that make it a versatile and convenient kitchen appliance:

> Dual Basket Technology

Equipped with two spacious 4.5 litres baskets, this air fryer offers exceptional versatility. You can choose to use a single basket for smaller portion cooking or harness the power of both baskets simultaneously to create wholesome, crispy meals with ease. With a combined 9 litres capacity, it can feed up to eight people at once. This means you can easily prepare meals for family gatherings or parties.

> Smart Finish Function with Match Cook

One of the standout features of this air fryer is the Smart Finish function. When cooking different foods with different cooking times in each basket, this function ensures that both baskets finish cooking at the same time. The Match Cook button is a handy addition that quickly sets both baskets to cook at the same temperature, simplifying the cooking process and ensuring consistent results.

> Versatile Cooking Options

The Tower Vortx Air Fryer goes beyond just air frying. It offers four different cooking methods, including air frying for crispy and healthy dishes, roasting for succulent chicken, pork, beef, or lamb, baking for cakes, tarts, or pies, and grilling with the crisper grill plate for juicy steaks. This versatility allows you to prepare a wide range of dishes with ease.

> 12 Pre-Set Meal Time Classics

To make cooking even more convenient, this air fryer provides 12 one-touch pre-set cooking options. These pre-sets take the guesswork out of cooking and ensure that your meals are perfectly cooked every time. Whether you are making fries, chicken, or desserts, you can rely on these pre-sets to achieve excellent results.

> Time-Saving and Healthier Cooking

Air frying technology allows you to enjoy your favourite fried foods with significantly less oil, making your meals healthier without sacrificing taste and texture. Additionally, the Smart Finish function and pre-set cooking options save you time in the kitchen, making meal preparation quick and hassle-free.

> Generous Capacity

With its 9 litres capacity, this air fryer is spacious enough to handle larger quantities of food, making it ideal for family meals, gatherings, or batch cooking. It eliminates the need to cook in multiple batches, saving you time and effort.

In short, the Tower Vortx Duo Basket Air Fryer offers versatility, convenience, and precision in cooking, making it a valuable addition to any kitchen. Whether you are cooking for a small family dinner or a large gathering, this air fryer provides the features and capacity to meet your culinary needs with ease.

How to Use the Tower Vortx Duo Basket Air Fryer?

To prepare your Tower Vortx Duo Basket Air Fryer for its initial use, start by unboxing the appliance and inspecting the cord and body for any damage. Dispose of the packaging responsibly and remove any stickers or labels from the unit, except for the rating label. Next, thoroughly clean the grill plates, baskets, and drawers using hot water, washing up liquid, and a non-abrasive sponge, ensuring they are completely dry before use. Place the grill plates at the bottom of the drawers. Wipe the inside and outside of the appliance with a damp cloth and ensure its dried thoroughly. Remember that this appliance operates with hot air and typically requires very little to no oil, so do not fill it with oil or frying fat. Familiarize yourself with the control panel as described in the Specifications section of the manual and position the appliance in accordance with the safety instructions provided. These steps will help ensure a safe and clean start when using your Tower Duo Basket Air Fryer.

Preparing For Use:

Ensure the appliance is placed on a stable, horizontal, and even surface, avoiding non-heat-resistant surfaces. Do not add any liquid or oil to the drawer. Keep the appliance clear of any obstructions on top to maintain proper airflow crucial for effective hot air frying. This appliance allows for the use of one or both drawers simultaneously. The Smart Finish function enables different foods with varying cooking times and temperatures to finish cooking at the same time.

Air Fryer Drawer Safety Switch:

To enhance safety, this air fryer features a built-in safety switch within the drawer, preventing unintended operation when the drawer is not correctly positioned or when the timer is left unset. Prior to use, always confirm that the grill plate is securely placed inside the drawer, and that the drawer is fully closed.

Using Your Appliance:

The control panel features various keys for functions, temperature and time adjustments, and preset menu selections. To remove the drawer, pull on the handle, but note that the unit will stop working if the drawer is removed during operation. It will resume upon reinsertion with the previous settings intact.

The Auto-Off Function:

When cooking is not in progress and there's no interaction with the control panel for 10 minutes, the appliance will automatically turn off. To manually turn off the unit during operation, press the ON/ Standby key.

Turning the Appliance ON/OFF:

Plug the unit into a mains socket, touch the ON/ Standby key to turn it on, and touch it again to stop operation. In the event of a power cut or unplugging during operation, the unit will continue with the previously set program upon reconnection.

Start/ Pause:

Once you have set the desired function, time, and temperature, touch the Start/Pause key to begin operation. You can pause and resume by using the same key.

Setting the Temperature:

The temperature control range is 50-200°C. Each touch of the Temperature +/- keys adjusts the temperature by 10°C increments. The display confirms the chosen setting with three flashes. Temperature can be changed during operation.

Setting the Timer:

The timer can be set from 1 to 60 minutes. Each touch of the Timer +/- keys adjusts the time by 1-minute increments. The display confirms the selected time with three flashes. Time adjustments can also be made during operation.

Pre-Set Menu Selection:

After placing food in the drawer(s), touch the drawer-specific key and then the desired cooking function icon. Adjust the temperature and time using the Temperature and Time keys if necessary. Start the operation by touching the Start/Pause key. When the timer ends, an audible signal will sound, and the unit will cool down for about 1 minute before entering standby mode. Check the readiness of your food and proceed accordingly.

Smart Finish:

The Smart Finish function in your dual-basket air fryer is a handy feature that allows you to cook different foods with varying cooking times and temperatures in each basket, while ensuring that both baskets finish cooking at the same time.

Match Cook:

When cooking the same food in both drawers, set one drawer as instructed above, and then select Match Cook for the other drawer, followed by touching the Start/Pause key.

Pre-Heat:

To pre-heat the appliance, select the desired drawer(s), choose the Pre-Heat function, and press the Start/Pause key. Pre-heating helps achieve a chargrill effect and added crispness to your dishes.

Cleaning and Maintenance

Proper cleaning and maintenance are essential to keep your appliance in good working condition and ensure safe, healthy cooking. Follow these cleaning and care instructions diligently:

1. Clean the appliance after every use to prevent the buildup of food residue and maintain optimal performance.

2. Before cleaning, switch off the appliance and unplug it from the wall socket. Allow the appliance to cool down, and for faster cooling, keep the drawers open to promote better airflow.

3. When cleaning the appliance, avoid using metal kitchen utensils or abrasive cleaning materials, as these can damage the non-stick coating and the appliance's surfaces.

4. To clean the drawer, basket, and grill plate, use hot water, a small amount of washing-up liquid, and a non-abrasive sponge or brush. This gentle cleaning method effectively removes food residues without harming the non-stick surfaces.

5. If stubborn food residue is stuck to the grill plate, basket, or the bottom of the drawer, consider soaking them in hot water and a bit of washing-up liquid for a few hours or overnight. This will help loosen the residue and make it easier to clean.

6. Ensure that water or any other liquid does not enter the unit while cleaning. This is crucial for the safety and functionality of the appliance.

7. Wipe the exterior of the appliance with a damp cloth to remove any splatters or residue on the outer surfaces.

8. Clean the heating element with a suitable cleaning brush to remove any food residues that may have accumulated during use. A clean heating element ensures efficient cooking and prevents potential smoke or odours.

9. Before using the appliance again, make sure that all cleaned parts are thoroughly dry. This helps prevent any potential safety hazards and ensures that your food cooks evenly.

*To store your appliance properly:
- Ensure that the air fryer is completely cool, clean, and dry before storing it.
- Store the appliance in a cool and dry place, away from direct sunlight and moisture. Proper storage prolongs the lifespan of your appliance and keeps it ready for the next use.

By following these cleaning and care instructions, you can enjoy safe, efficient, and long-lasting performance from your air fryer while maintaining the quality and flavour of your cooked meals.

FAQS

1. What is a dual basket air fryer, and how does it work?

A dual basket air fryer is an appliance that allows you to cook two different dishes simultaneously in separate baskets. It works by circulating hot air around the food, cooking it evenly and providing a crispy texture, similar to deep frying but with little to no oil.

2. What are the advantages of using a dual basket air fryer?

The main advantage is the ability to cook two different dishes at the same time, saving you time and effort. It's also versatile, allowing you to prepare a variety of foods with less oil for a healthier cooking option.

3. Can I use only one basket if I don't need both at the same time?

Yes, most dual basket air fryers allow you to use just one basket when needed. This flexibility is especially useful for smaller meals or when you want to cook different dishes sequentially.

4. How do I clean a dual basket air fryer?

Typically, you can remove the baskets and other removable parts for easy cleaning. Use hot, soapy water and a non-abrasive sponge or brush to clean them. Make sure all parts are dry before reassembling and using the appliance again.

5. Is it safe to cook different foods with different cooking times in each basket?

Yes, many dual baskets air fryers come equipped with a Smart Finish function that ensures both baskets finish cooking at the same time, even if they have different cooking times and temperatures.

6. Can I cook frozen foods directly in the air fryer?

Yes, you can cook frozen foods in a dual basket air fryer. Just follow the recommended time and temperature settings provided in the appliance's manual or on the packaging of the frozen food.

7. What types of dishes can I prepare in a dual basket air fryer?

You can prepare a wide variety of dishes, including but not limited to, French fries, chicken wings, fish fillets, vegetables, cakes, steaks, and more. Many air fryers also come with pre-set cooking options for specific dishes.

8. Do I need to preheat the dual basket air fryer before cooking?

Preheating is optional and depends on your preference. Preheating can help achieve a crisper texture in some dishes, but it's not always necessary.

9. Can I use aluminium foil or parchment paper in the baskets?

Yes, you can use aluminium foil or parchment paper in the baskets to prevent food from sticking. However, ensure there's enough space for proper air circulation and avoid covering the entire surface.

10. Is it possible to adjust the cooking temperature and time during the cooking process?

Yes, most dual basket air fryers allow you to adjust the cooking temperature and time while the appliance is in operation. This flexibility lets you fine-tune your cooking to achieve the desired results.

CHAPTER 2
Breakfast

Healthy Banana Bread

MAKES 2 LOAVES

| **PREP TIME:** 10 minutes
| **COOK TIME:** 22 minutes

cooking spray
2 ripe bananas, mashed
200 g sugar
140 g plain flour
1 large egg
60 g unsalted butter, melted
5 g baking soda
1 tsp. salt

1. Spray the insides of 2 mini loaf pans with cooking spray.
2. In a large mixing bowl, mix the bananas and sugar and combine well.
3. In a separate large mixing bowl, mix the egg, butter, flour, baking soda, and salt and stir well.
4. Transfer the banana mixture to the egg mixture. Mix well.
5. Divide the batter evenly among the prepared pans.
6. When ready to cook, remove the grill plates and preheat the airfryer baskets for three minutes by activating the automatic preheat key.
7. Place 1 loaf pan in each basket. Select the Match Cook key then set basket 1 to 180°C for 22 minutes, then touch the start key to activate the airfryer. Bake until toothpick inserted in centre comes out clean.
8. When the cooking is complete, turn out the loaves onto a wire rack to cool. Serve warm.

Veggies Omelette

SERVES 2

| **PREP TIME:** 10 minutes
| **COOK TIME:** 13 minutes

10 ml rapeseed oil
4 eggs, whisked
1 white onion, finely chopped
1 red bell pepper, seeded and chopped
1 green bell pepper, seeded and chopped
50 g baby spinach leaves, roughly chopped
50 g Halloumi cheese, shaved
45 ml plain milk
5 g melted butter
Salt and freshly ground black pepper, to taste

1. Grease a 18 x 13-cm baking pan with rapeseed oil.
2. Place the remaining ingredients in the greased baking pan and mix well.
3. When ready to cook, remove the grill plate from basket 1 then pre-heat the airfryer basket for three minutes by activating the automatic preheat key.
4. Put the baking pan into basket 1 and set the temperature to 180°C for 13 minutes, then touch the start key to activate the airfryer.
5. When cooking is complete, remove the omelette from the airfryer and serve warm.

Potato and Kale Nuggets

SERVES 4

| PREP TIME: 10 minutes
| COOK TIME: 18 minutes

Cooking spray
5 ml extra virgin olive oil
400 g potatoes, boiled and mashed
300 g kale, rinsed and chopped
30 ml milk
1 clove garlic, minced
Salt and ground black pepper, to taste

1. In a frying pan over medium heat, sauté the garlic with the olive oil, until it turns golden brown. Add the kale and cook for an additional 3 minutes and remove from the heat.
2. Mix the mashed potatoes, kale and garlic in a medium bowl. Pour in the milk and sprinkle with salt and pepper to taste.
3. Shape the mixture into nuggets and spray with cooking spray.
4. When ready to cook, remove the grill plate from basket 1 then preheat the airfryer basket for three minutes by activating the automatic preheat key.
5. Put the nuggets into basket 1 and set the temperature to 200°C for 15 minutes, then touch the start key to activate the airfryer. Halfway through cooking, carefully flip the nuggets over.
6. When cooking is complete, transfer the nuggets to a plate. Serve warm.

Nut and Seed Muffins

MAKES 8 MUFFINS

| PREP TIME: 15 minutes
| COOK TIME: 14 minutes

Cooking spray
95 g whole-wheat flour
120 ml buttermilk
30 g melted butter
50 g brown sugar
50 g grated carrots
25 g oat bran
20 g flaxseed meal
2 g baking soda
2 g baking powder

¼ tsp. salt
½ tsp. cinnamon
1 egg
25 g chopped pecans
25 g chopped walnuts
10 g pumpkin seeds
10 g sunflower seeds
½ tsp. pure vanilla extract
Special Equipment:
16 foil muffin cups, paper liners removed

1. In a large bowl, stir together the flour, flaxseed meal, bran, sugar, baking soda, baking powder, salt and cinnamon.
2. In a medium bowl, beat together the buttermilk, egg, butter and vanilla. Pour the egg mixture into flour mixture and stir just until dry ingredients moisten. Do not beat.
3. Gently stir in the carrots, nuts and seeds.
4. Double up the foil cups so you have 8 total and spray with cooking spray.
5. When ready to cook, remove the grill plates and preheat the airfryer baskets for three minutes by activating the automatic preheat key.
6. Place 4 foil cups in a single layer in each basket. Select the Match Cook key then set basket 1 to 165°C for 14 minutes, then touch the start key to activate the airfryer. Bake until a toothpick inserted in centre comes out clean.
7. When cooking is complete, serve warm.

Cornflakes Toast Sticks

SERVES 4

| PREP TIME: 10 minutes
| COOK TIME: 8 minutes

Cooking spray
2 eggs
80 g crushed cornflakes
120 ml milk
6 slices sandwich bread, each slice cut into 4 strips
⅛ tsp. salt
½ tsp. pure vanilla extract
Maple syrup, for dipping

1. In a small bowl, beat together the eggs, milk, vanilla and salt.
2. Put the crushed cornflakes on a plate.
3. Dip the bread strips in egg mixture, shake off excess, and roll in cornflake crumbs.
4. Spray both sides of bread strips with cooking spray.
5. When ready to cook, remove the grill plates and preheat the airfryer baskets for three minutes by activating the automatic preheat key.
6. Place half of the bread strips in a single layer in each basket. Select the Match Cook key then set basket 1 to 200°C for 8 minutes, then touch the start key to activate the airfryer. For even browning carefully flip the bread strips over halfway through cooking using a silicone spatula.
7. When cooking is complete, transfer the bread strips to a plate. Serve warm with maple syrup.

Creamy Cinnamon Doughnuts

SERVES 8

| PREP TIME: 10 minutes
| COOK TIME: 16 minutes

cooking spray
60 g butter, softened and divided
100 g sugar
75 g caster sugar
120 g sour cream
2 large egg yolks

350 g plain flour
7 g baking powder
1 pinch baking soda
2 g cinnamon
1 tsp. salt

1. Mix together sugar and butter in a medium bowl and beat until crumbly mixture is formed.
2. Whisk in the egg yolks and beat until combined well.
3. Sift together flour, baking powder, baking soda and salt in another bowl.
4. Add the flour mixture and sour cream to the sugar mixture.
5. Mix well to form a dough and refrigerate it.
6. Roll the dough into 5 cm thickness and cut the dough in half.
7. Brush both sides of the dough with the melted butter.
8. When ready to cook, remove the grill plates and preheat the airfryer baskets for three minutes by activating the automatic preheat key.
9. Spray with cooking spray and place one dough in each basket. Select the Match Cook key then set basket 1 to 180°C for 16 minutes, then touch the start key to activate the airfryer.
10. When cooking is complete, sprinkle the doughnuts with the cinnamon and caster sugar to serve.

Classic British Breakfast

SERVES 2

| PREP TIME: 5 minutes
| COOK TIME: 20 minutes

15 ml olive oil
2 eggs
240 g potatoes, sliced and diced
400 g baked beans
1 sausage
Salt, to taste

1. Break the eggs onto a 18 x 13-cm baking dish and sprinkle with salt to taste.
2. Lay the baked beans on the dish, next to the eggs.
3. In a medium bowl, coat the potatoes with the olive oil. Sprinkle with salt.
4. Remove the grill plates from both baskets then preheat the airfryer baskets for three minutes by activating the automatic preheat key.
5. Transfer the potato slices to basket 1, set the temperature to 200°C for 20 minutes; next add the dish to basket 2, set the temperature to 190°C for 16 minutes. Select the Smart Finish key then touch the start key to activate the airfryer.
6. When the dish has been cooking for 11 minutes, slice up the sausage and throw the slices on top of the beans and eggs. Cook for a further 5 minutes until the sausage is cooked.
7. When cooking is complete, transfer to a plate and serve immediately.

Honey Oat and Chia Porridge

SERVES 4

| PREP TIME: 10 minutes
| COOK TIME: 8 minutes

30 g peanut butter
200 g oats
160 g chia seeds

960 ml milk
60 ml honey
15 g butter, melted

1. Place the peanut butter, honey, butter and milk in a bowl and stir to mix well. Add the oats and chia seeds and stir well.
2. Transfer the oat mixture to two 18 x 13-cm baking dish.
3. When ready to cook, remove the grill plates and preheat the airfryer baskets for three minutes by activating the automatic preheat key.
4. Place one baking dish in each basket. Select the Match Cook key then set basket 1 to 200°C for 8 minutes, then touch the start key to activate the airfryer.
5. When cooking is complete, give another stir before serving.

Gold Avocado

SERVES 4

| PREP TIME: 5 minutes
| COOK TIME: 8 minutes

2 large avocados, sliced
2 eggs, beaten
100 g breadcrumbs
60 g wholemeal flour
¼ tsp. paprika
Salt and ground black pepper, to taste

1. Sprinkle the paprika, salt and pepper on the slices of avocado.
2. Lightly coat the avocados with flour. Dredge them in the eggs, before covering with breadcrumbs.
3. When ready to cook, remove the grill plate from basket 1 then preheat the airfryer basket for three minutes by activating the automatic preheat key.
4. Put the avocados into basket 1 and set the temperature to 200°C for 8 minutes, then touch the start key to activate the airfryer. Halfway through cooking, carefully flip the avocados over.
5. When cooking is complete, transfer the avocados to a plate. Serve warm.

Egg in a Bread Basket

SERVES 2

| PREP TIME: 10 minutes
| COOK TIME: 12 minutes

7 ml olive oil
2 bread slices
2 eggs
1 rasher of bacon, chopped
4 tomato slices
15 g Mozzarella cheese, shredded
30 ml mayonnaise
⅛ tsp. maple syrup
⅛ tsp. balsamic vinegar
¼ tsp. fresh parsley, chopped
Salt and black pepper, to taste

1. Grease two 10 cm ramekins lightly.
2. Place 1 bread slice in each prepared ramekin and add the bacon and tomato slices.
3. Top with the Mozzarella cheese evenly and crack 1 egg in each ramekin.
4. Drizzle with balsamic vinegar and maple syrup and season with fresh parsley, salt and black pepper.
5. When ready to cook, remove the grill plates and preheat the airfryer baskets for three minutes by activating the automatic preheat key.
6. Place one ramekin in each basket. Select the Match Cook key then set basket 1 to 160°C for 12 minutes, then touch the start key to activate the airfryer.
7. When cooking is complete, top with mayonnaise and serve warm.

Spanish Style Frittata

SERVES 2

| PREP TIME: 10 minutes
| COOK TIME: 14 minutes

15 ml olive oil
1 potato, boiled, peeled and cubed
60 g frozen corn
3 jumbo eggs
½ of chorizo sausage, sliced
30 g feta cheese, crumbled
Salt and black pepper, to taste

1. Grease a 18 x 13 cm baking pan with olive oil.
2. Add the chorizo sausage, corn and potato in the baking pan.
3. When ready to cook, remove the grill plate from basket 1 then preheat the airfryer basket for three minutes by activating the automatic preheat key.
4. Put the pan into basket 1 and set the temperature to 180°C for 14 minutes, then touch the start key to activate the airfryer.
5. When the frittata has been cooking for 9 minutes, pour the eggs over the sausage mixture and top with feta cheese. Cook for a further 5 minutes until the cheese is melted.
6. When cooking is complete, transfer the frittata to a plate and serve warm.

CHAPTER 3
Pork

BBQ Pork Ribs with Green Beans

SERVES 4

| PREP TIME: 5 minutes
| COOK TIME: 30 minutes

5 ml sesame oil
1 tbsp. barbecue dry rub
450 g pork ribs, chopped
450 g green beans, trimmed and halved
5 g mustard
15 ml apple cider vinegar
5 g unsalted butter, melted
¼ tsp. garlic powder

1. Combine the dry rub, apple cider vinegar, mustard and sesame oil, then coat the ribs with this mixture. Refrigerate the ribs for about 20 minutes.
2. Mix the green beans, butter and garlic powder in a medium bowl and toss to coat well.
3. When ready to cook, remove the grill plate from basket 2 then preheat the airfryer baskets for three minutes by activating the automatic preheat key.
4. Place the ribs onto the grill plate in basket 1 and set the temperature to 190°C for 30 minutes. Put the green beans into basket 2 and set the temperature to 200°C for 15 minutes, then activate the Smart Finish key and touch the start key to activate the airfryer. Halfway through cooking, flip the ribs over and give the green beans a shake.
5. When cooking is complete, serve the ribs with green beans.

Bacon Wrapped Pork Tenderloin

SERVES 4

| PREP TIME: 15 minutes
| COOK TIME: 30 minutes

1 (680 g) pork tenderloin
4 rashers of bacon
30 g Dijon mustard

1. Rub the tenderloin evenly with the mustard and wrap with rashers of bacon.
2. Preheat the basket 1 with the grill plate inserted for three minutes by activating the automatic preheat key.
3. Place the pork tenderloin into basket 1 and set the temperature to 190°C for 30 minutes then touch the start key to activate the airfryer. Halfway through cooking, flip the pork tenderloin over.
4. When cooking is complete, transfer the pork tenderloin to a plate. Cut into desired size slices to serve.

Mexican Pork Chops

SERVES 2

| PREP TIME: 5 minutes
| COOK TIME: 16 minutes

¼ tsp. dried oregano
2 (115 g) boneless pork chops
30 g unsalted butter, divided
1½ tsps. taco seasoning mix

1. Combine the dried oregano and taco seasoning in a small bowl and rub this mixture into the pork chops. Brush the pork chops with 1 tbsp. butter.
2. Preheat the basket 1 with the grill plate inserted for three minutes by activating the automatic preheat key.
3. Place the pork chops into basket 1 and set the temperature to 190°C for 16 minutes then touch the start key to activate the airfryer. Half-way through cooking, flip the pork chops over.
4. When cooking is complete, transfer the pork chops to a plate. Serve with a garnish of remaining butter.

Cheese Bacon Wrapped Jalapeño Poppers

SERVES 6

| PREP TIME: 5 minutes
| COOK TIME: 16 minutes

6 large jalapeños
115 g ⅓-less-fat cream cheese
6 rashers of middle bacon, halved
30 g shredded reduced-fat sharp Cheddar cheese
2 spring onions, green tops only, sliced

1. Wearing rubber gloves, halve the jalapeños lengthwise to make 12 pieces. Scoop out the seeds and membranes and discard.
2. In a medium bowl, mix the cream cheese, Cheddar and spring onions and combine well.
3. Using a small spoon or spatula, fill the jalapeños with the cream cheese filling. Wrap a rasher of bacon around each pepper and secure with a toothpick.
4. When ready to cook, remove the grill plates and preheat the airfryer baskets for three minutes by activating the automatic preheat key.
5. Place half of stuffed peppers in a single layer in each basket. Select the Match Cook key then set basket 1 to 200°C for 16 minutes, then touch the start key to activate the airfryer. Cook until the peppers are tender, the bacon is browned and crisp, and the cheese is melted.
6. When cooking is complete, transfer the stuffed peppers to a plate. Serve warm.

Garlic Butter Pork Chops

SERVES 4

| PREP TIME: 10 minutes
| COOK TIME: 20 minutes

15 ml coconut oil
4 pork chops
15 g coconut butter
2 g parsley
2 tsps. garlic, grated
Salt and black pepper, to taste

1. Mix all the seasonings, garlic, coconut oil, coconut butter and parsley in a bowl and coat the pork chops with it.
2. Cover the pork chops with foil and refrigerate to marinate for about 1 hour.
3. Preheat the airfryer baskets with the grill plates inserted for three minutes by activating the automatic preheat key.
4. Remove the foil and arrange 2 chops in a single layer in each basket. Select the Match Cook key and set basket 1 to 190°C for 20 minutes and touch the start key to activate.
5. For even browning, carefully flip the chops over halfway through cooking using a silicone spatula.
6. When cooking is complete, transfer the pork chops to a plate. Serve warm.

Homemade Sausage Meatballs

SERVES 4

| PREP TIME: 15 minutes
| COOK TIME: 14 minutes

cooking spray
100 g sausage, casing removed
½ medium onion, minced finely
18 g Italian breadcrumbs
1 tsp. fresh sage, chopped finely
½ tsp. garlic, minced
Salt and black pepper, to taste

1. Mix all the ingredients in a small bowl until well combined.
2. Shape this mixture into equal-sized balls.
3. When ready to cook, remove the grill plate from basket 1 then preheat the airfryer basket for three minutes by activating the automatic preheat key.
4. Put the balls into basket 1 and lightly spray with the cooking spray. Set the temperature to 200°C for 14 minutes, then touch the start key to activate the airfryer. Halfway through cooking, carefully turn the balls over.
5. When cooking is complete, transfer the balls to a plate and serve warm.

Caramelised Pork

SERVES 6

| PREP TIME: 10 minutes
| COOK TIME: 18 minutes

900 g pork shoulder, cut into 4-cm thick slices
30 g sugar
80 ml soy sauce
15 ml honey

1. Mix all the ingredients in a large bowl and coat the pork well.
2. Cover and refrigerate for about 8 hours.
3. Preheat the airfryer baskets with the grill plates inserted for three minutes by activating the automatic preheat key.
4. Place half of pork slices into each basket. Select the Match Cook key and set basket 1 to 190°C for 18 minutes and touch the start key to activate. Halfway through cooking, carefully flip the pork over.
5. When cooking is complete, transfer the pork to a plate and serve warm.

Pork Tenderloin and Veggies

SERVES 3

| PREP TIME: 20 minutes
| COOK TIME: 40 minutes

30 ml olive oil
3 potatoes
3 (170 g) pork tenderloins
340 g frozen green beans
6 rashers of bacon

1. Pierce the potatoes with a fork.
2. Wrap 4-6 green beans with one rasher of bacon and coat the pork tenderloins evenly with olive oil.
3. When ready to cook, remove the grill plate from basket 1, then preheat the airfryer baskets for three minutes by activating the automatic preheat key.
4. Transfer the potatoes into basket 1, set the temperature to 200°C and for 40 minutes then carefully place the pork tenderloins onto the grill plate in basket 2, set the temperature to 190°C and for 25 minutes. Then touch the start key to activate the airfryer.
5. When the pork tenderloins are cooked, gently transfer to a serving dish and cut into desired size slices.
6. Arrange the bean rolls in basket 2, set temperature to 200°C and for 15 minutes.
7. When cooking is complete, transfer the potatoes and bean rolls to a plate. Serve warm with the pork tenderloins.

Citrus Pork Loin Roast

SERVES 8

| PREP TIME: 10 minutes
| COOK TIME: 40 minutes

Cooking spray
15 ml lime juice
900 g boneless pork loin roast
20 g orange marmalade
1 tsp. dried lemongrass
1 tsp. coarse brown mustard
1 tsp. curry powder
Salt and ground black pepper, to taste

1. Mix the lime juice, marmalade, mustard, lemongrass and curry powder.
2. Rub the mixture all over the surface of the pork loin. Season with salt and pepper to taste.
3. Preheat the basket 1 with the grill plate inserted for three minutes by activating the automatic preheat key.
4. Place the pork roast diagonally into basket 1 and spray with cooking spray. Set the temperature to 190°C for 40 minutes, then touch the start key to activate the airfryer.
5. When cooking is complete, wrap the roast in foil and let rest for about 10 minutes before slicing.

Breaded Pork Chops and Parsnips

SERVES 2

| PREP TIME: 15 minutes
| COOK TIME: 30 minutes

15 ml vegetable oil
2 (170 g) pork chops
30 g plain flour
1 egg
115 g breadcrumbs
300 g parsnips, peeled and cut into 2.5 cm chunks
15 g butter, melted
Salt and black pepper, to taste

1. Mix the parsnips and butter in a medium bowl and toss to coat well.
2. Season the pork chops with salt and black pepper to taste.
3. Place the flour in a shallow bowl and whisk an egg in a second bowl.
4. Mix the breadcrumbs and vegetable oil in a third bowl.
5. Coat the pork chops with flour, dip into egg and dredge into the breadcrumb mixture.
6. When ready to cook, remove the grill plate from basket 1, then preheat the airfryer baskets for three minutes by activating the automatic preheat key.
7. Transfer the parsnips into basket 1, set the temperature to 200°C and for 30 minutes then carefully place the chops onto the grill plate in basket 2, set the temperature to 190°C and for 18 minutes.
8. Select the Smart Finish key then touch the start key to activate the airfryer. Halfway through cooking, give the parsnips a shake and flip the pork chops over.
9. When cooking is complete, serve the chops warm with parsnips.

Glazed Ham

SERVES 4

| PREP TIME: 10 minutes
| COOK TIME: 30 minutes

1 (450 g) ham joint
180 ml whiskey
30 ml honey
30 g French mustard

1. Mix all the ingredients in a medium bowl except ham.
2. Keep ham joint for about 30 minutes at room temperature.
3. Preheat the basket 1 with the grill plate inserted for three minutes by activating the automatic preheat key.
4. Place ham joint into basket 1 and top with half of the whiskey mixture. Set the temperature to 200°C for 30 minutes, then touch the start key to activate the airfryer. Halfway through cooking, flip the ham joint over and coat with the remaining whiskey mixture.
5. When cooking is complete, transfer the ham joint to a plate and serve hot.

CHAPTER 4
Vegetable

Broccoli with Cauliflower

SERVES 4

| PREP TIME: 15 minutes
| COOK TIME: 20 minutes

30 ml olive oil, divided
180 g cauliflower, cut into 2.5 cm pieces
180 g broccoli, cut into 2.5 cm pieces
Salt, as required

1. Mix the cauliflower, 15 ml olive oil and salt in a small bowl and toss to coat well.
2. Combine the broccoli, remaining olive oil and salt in another bowl and toss to coat well.
3. Remove the grill plates from both baskets then preheat the airfryer baskets for three minutes by activating the automatic preheat key.
4. Transfer the broccoli to basket 1, set the temperature to 200°C for 14 minutes; next add the cauliflower to basket 2, set the temperature to 200°C for 20 minutes. Select the Smart Finish key then touch the start key to activate the airfryer. Shake both baskets halfway through cooking.
5. When cooking is complete, transfer the vegetables to a plate and serve immediately.

Crispy Bacon-Wrapped Asparagus Bundles

SERVES 4

| PREP TIME: 20 minutes
| COOK TIME: 12 minutes

12 ml olive oil
450 g asparagus
4 rashers of bacon
22 g brown sugar
5 g sesame seeds, toasted
1 garlic clove, minced
7 ml sesame oil

1. Mix the garlic, brown sugar, olive oil and sesame oil in a small bowl until sugar is dissolved.
2. Divide the asparagus into 4 equal bunches and wrap a rasher of bacon around each bunch.
3. Rub the asparagus bunch evenly with the garlic mixture.
4. When ready to cook, remove the grill plate from basket 1 then preheat the airfryer basket for three minutes by activating the automatic preheat key.
5. Put the asparagus bunches into basket 1 and sprinkle with sesame seeds. Set the temperature to 200°C for 12 minutes then touch the start key to activate the airfryer. Halfway through cooking, carefully flip the asparagus bunches over.
6. When cooking is complete, transfer the asparagus bunches to a plate. Serve warm.

Almond Asparagus

SERVES 3

| PREP TIME: 15 minutes
| COOK TIME: 12 minutes

30 ml olive oil
450 g asparagus
30 ml balsamic vinegar
40 g almonds, sliced
Salt and black pepper, to taste

1. Mix the asparagus, olive oil, vinegar, salt and black pepper in a bowl and toss to coat well.
2. When ready to cook, remove the grill plate from basket 1 then pre-heat the airfryer basket for three minutes by activating the automatic preheat key.
3. Place asparagus and sprinkle the almond slices into basket 1 and set the temperature to 200°C for 12 minutes, then touch the start key to activate the airfryer. Halfway through cooking, carefully flip the asparagus over.
4. When cooking is complete, transfer the asparagus to a plate. Serve warm.

Caramelised Baby Carrots

SERVES 3

| PREP TIME: 10 minutes
| COOK TIME: 15 minutes

100 g brown sugar
1 small bag baby carrots
110 g butter, melted

1. Mix the butter and brown sugar in a medium bowl.
2. Add the carrots and toss to coat evenly.
3. When ready to cook, remove the grill plate from basket 1 then pre-heat the airfryer basket for three minutes by activating the automatic preheat key.
4. Put the carrots into basket 1 and set the temperature to 200°C for 15 minutes, then touch the start key to activate the airfryer. Halfway through cooking, carefully flip the carrots over.
5. When cooking is complete, transfer the carrots to a plate. Serve warm.

Breadcrumbs Stuffed Mushrooms

SERVES 4

| PREP TIME: 15 minutes
| COOK TIME: 15 minutes

22 ml olive oil
1½ spelt bread slices
16 small button mushrooms, stemmed and gills removed
2 g flat-leaf parsley, finely chopped
1 garlic clove, crushed
Salt and black pepper, to taste

1. Place the bread slices in a food processor and pulse until fine crumbs form.
2. Transfer the crumbs into a small bowl and stir in the olive oil, garlic, parsley, salt and pepper.
3. Evenly stuff the breadcrumbs mixture in each mushroom cap.
4. When ready to cook, remove the grill plates and preheat the airfryer baskets for three minutes by activating the automatic preheat key.
5. Place half of mushroom caps in a single layer in each basket. Select the Match Cook key then set basket 1 to 200°C for 15 minutes, then touch the start key to activate the airfryer.
6. When cooking is complete, transfer the mushroom caps to a plate. Serve hot.

Spices Stuffed Aubergines

SERVES 4

| PREP TIME: 15 minutes
| COOK TIME: 15 minutes

20 ml olive oil, divided
8 baby aubergines
¾ tbsp. ground coriander
¾ tbsp. dry mango powder
1 g ground turmeric
1 g ground cumin
1 g garlic powder
Salt, to taste

1. Make 2 slits from the bottom of each aubergine leaving the stems intact.
2. Add 5 ml olive oil, mango powder, coriander, cumin, turmeric and garlic powder in a small bowl, mix well.
3. Fill each slit of aubergines with this spices mixture. Brush the outer side of each aubergine with remaining olive oil.
4. When ready to cook, remove the grill plates and preheat the airfryer baskets for three minutes by activating the automatic preheat key.
5. Place half of the aubergines in a single layer in each basket. Select the Match Cook key then set basket 1 to 190°C for 15 minutes, then touch the start key to activate the airfryer.
6. When cooking is complete, transfer the aubergines to a plate. Serve hot.

Cheese Bell Peppers Cups

SERVES 4

| PREP TIME: 10 minutes
| COOK TIME: 15 minutes

7 ml olive oil
8 mini red bell peppers, tops and seeds removed
90 g feta cheese, crumbled
1 g fresh parsley, chopped
Freshly ground black pepper, to taste

1. Mix the feta cheese, parsley, olive oil and black pepper in a bowl.
2. Stuff the bell peppers with the feta cheese mixture.
3. When ready to cook, remove the grill plates and preheat the airfryer baskets for three minutes by activating the automatic preheat key.
4. Place 4 bell peppers in a single layer in each basket. Select the Match Cook key then set basket 1 to 200°C for 15 minutes, then touch the start key to activate the airfryer.
5. When cooking is complete, transfer the bell peppers to a plate. Serve hot.

Favourite Potatoes

SERVES 4

| PREP TIME: 10 minutes
| COOK TIME: 22 minutes

800 g waxy potatoes, cubed and boiled
120 ml Greek plain yoghurt
30 ml olive oil, divided
1 tbsp. paprika, divided
Salt and black pepper, to taste

1. Mix 15 ml olive oil, ⅓ tbsp. of paprika, black pepper and maxy potatoes in a large bowl and toss to coat well.
2. When ready to cook, remove the grill plate from basket 1 then preheat the airfryer basket for three minutes by activating the automatic preheat key.
3. Put the potatoes into basket 1 and set the temperature to 200°C for 22 minutes, then touch the start key to activate the airfryer. Halfway through cooking, carefully shake for 10 seconds.
4. When cooking is complete, transfer the potatoes to a plate. Mix the yoghurt, remaining olive oil, salt and black pepper in a bowl and serve with potatoes.

Balsamic Brussels Sprouts

SERVES 3

| PREP TIME: 15 minutes
| COOK TIME: 18 minutes

15 ml extra-virgin olive oil
450 g Brussels sprouts, trimmed and halved
30 g Parmesan cheese, shredded
40 g whole wheat breadcrumbs
15 ml balsamic vinegar
Salt and black pepper, to taste

1. Mix the Brussels sprouts, vinegar, olive oil, salt and black pepper in a medium bowl and toss to coat well.
2. When ready to cook, remove the grill plate from basket 1 then preheat the airfryer basket for three minutes by activating the automatic preheat key.
3. Put the Brussels sprouts into basket 1 and set the temperature to 200°C for 18 minutes, then touch the start key to activate the airfryer.
4. When the Brussels sprouts have been cooking for 13 minutes, sprinkle with breadcrumbs and cheese. Cook for a further 5 minutes until the cheese is melted.
5. When cooking is complete, transfer the Brussels sprouts to a plate. Serve hot.

Courgette and Spinach Salad

SERVES 4

| PREP TIME: 15 minutes
| COOK TIME: 18 minutes

30 ml olive oil
450 g courgette, cut into rounds
500 g fresh spinach, chopped
30 g feta cheese, crumbled
1 tsp. garlic powder
Salt and black pepper, as required
30 ml fresh lemon juice

1. Mix the courgette, olive oil, garlic powder, salt and black pepper in a medium bowl and toss to coat well.
2. When ready to cook, remove the grill plate from basket 1 then preheat the airfryer basket for three minutes by activating the automatic preheat key.
3. Put the courgette slices into basket 1 and set the temperature to 200°C for 18 minutes, then touch the start key to activate the airfryer. Halfway through cooking, carefully flip the courgette slices over.
4. When cooking is complete, transfer the courgette slices to a plate and keep aside to cool.
5. Add the spinach, feta cheese, lemon juice, a little bit of salt and black pepper and mix well. Toss to coat well and enjoy.

Radish and Mozzarella Salad

SERVES 4

| PREP TIME: 15 minutes
| COOK TIME: 30 minutes

30 ml olive oil
680 g radishes, trimmed and halved
5 ml honey
225 g fresh mozzarella, sliced
Salt and freshly ground black pepper, to taste

1. Mix the radishes, mozzarella, salt, black pepper and olive oil in a large bowl and toss to coat well.
2. When ready to cook, remove the grill plate from basket 1 then preheat the airfryer basket for three minutes by activating the automatic preheat key.
3. Put the radishes into basket 1 and set the temperature to 190°C for 30 minutes, then touch the start key to activate the airfryer. Halfway through cooking, carefully flip the radishes over.
4. When cooking is complete, transfer the radishes to a plate. Top with the honey and serve immediately.

CHAPTER 5

Beef

Avocado Buttered Flank Steak

SERVES 1

| PREP TIME: 5 minutes
| COOK TIME: 12 minutes

1 flank steak
2 avocados
120 ml chimichurri sauce
30 g butter, melted
Salt and ground black pepper, to taste

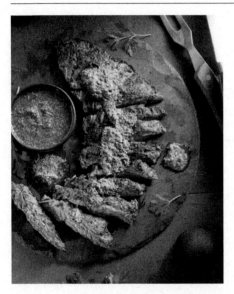

1. Rub the flank steak with salt and pepper and leave to stand for about 20 minutes.
2. Halve the avocados and take out the pits. Spoon the flesh into a small bowl and mash with a fork. Mix in the melted butter and chimichurri sauce, making sure everything is well combined.
3. Preheat the basket 1 with the grill plate inserted for three minutes by activating the automatic preheat key.
4. Place the steak into basket 1 and set the temperature to 200°C for 12 minutes then touch the start key to activate the airfryer. Halfway through cooking, flip the steak over.
5. When cooking is complete, transfer the steak to a plate. Serve with the avocado butter.

Homemade Mushroom and Beef Meatloaf

SERVES 4

| PREP TIME: 10 minutes
| COOK TIME: 25 minutes

450 g minced beef
120 g mushrooms, sliced
1 egg, beaten
15 g bread crumbs
1 tbsp. thyme
1 small onion, chopped
Ground black pepper, to taste

1. Add all the ingredients in a large bowl and combine evenly.
2. Transfer the meatloaf mixture into the loaf pan.
3. When ready to cook, remove the grill plate from basket 1 then preheat the airfryer basket for three minutes by activating the automatic preheat key.
4. Put the loaf pan into basket 1 and set the temperature to 200°C for 25 minutes, then touch the start key to activate the airfryer. Bake until toothpick inserted in centre comes out clean.
5. When cooking is complete, remove the meatloaf from the airfryer. Cut into desired size slices and serve.

Chinese-style Beef Short Ribs

SERVES 8

| PREP TIME: 15 minutes
| COOK TIME: 20 minutes

1.8 kg bone-in beef short ribs
80 g spring onions, chopped
240 ml low-sodium soy sauce
120 ml rice vinegar
28 g brown sugar
15 ml Sriracha
1 tbsp. fresh ginger, finely grated
1 tsp. ground black pepper

1. Put the beef ribs with all other ingredients in a resealable bag and seal the bag.
2. Shake to coat well and refrigerate overnight.
3. Preheat the airfryer baskets with the grill plates inserted for three minutes by activating the automatic preheat key.
4. Remove the short ribs from resealable bag and arrange half of the ribs in a single layer into each basket. Select the Match Cook key and set basket 1 to 200°C for 20 minutes and touch the start key to activate.
5. For even browning, carefully flip the ribs over halfway through cooking using a silicone spatula.
6. When cooking is complete, transfer the ribs to a plate. Serve hot.

Simple Filet Mignon

SERVES 4

| PREP TIME: 10 minutes
| COOK TIME: 15 minutes

15 g butter, softened
2 (170 g) filet mignon steaks
Salt and black pepper, to taste

1. Rub the steaks generously with salt and black pepper and coat evenly with butter.
2. Preheat the basket 1 with the grill plate inserted for three minutes by activating the automatic preheat key.
3. Place the steaks into basket 1 and set the temperature to 200°C for 15 minutes then touch the start key to activate the airfryer. Halfway through cooking, flip the steaks over.
4. When cooking is complete, transfer the steaks to a plate and cut into desired size slices to serve.

Beef Braising Cheeseburgers

SERVES 4

| PREP TIME: 10 minutes
| COOK TIME: 12 minutes

340 g beef braising steak, minced
1 envelope onion soup mix
4 slices Cheddar cheese
4 ciabatta rolls
1 tsp. paprika
coarse salt and freshly ground black pepper, to taste

1. In a medium bowl, stir together the minced braising steak, onion soup mix, salt, black pepper, and paprika and combine well.
2. Divide the mixture into four equal portions and mould each one into a patty.
3. Preheat the airfryer baskets with the grill plates inserted for three minutes by activating the automatic preheat key.
4. Carefully place 2 patties in a single layer into each basket. Select the Match Cook key and set basket 1 to 200°C for 12 minutes and touch the start key to activate.
5. When the patties has been cooking for 11 minutes, top with the slices of cheese on the top of the patties. Cook for a further 1 minute until the cheese is melted.
6. When cooking is complete, transfer the patties to a plate. Serve warm on ciabatta rolls.

Herbed Beef Roast

SERVES 5

| PREP TIME: 10 minutes
| COOK TIME: 45 minutes

15 ml olive oil
900 g beef roast
1 tsp. dried thyme, crushed
1 tsp. dried rosemary, crushed
Salt, to taste

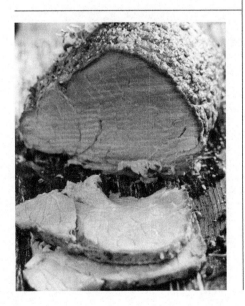

1. Mix the herbs and salt in a small bowl.
2. Rub the roast generously with the herb mixture and coat with olive oil.
3. Preheat the basket 1 with the grill plate inserted for three minutes by activating the automatic preheat key.
4. Place the roast into basket 1 and set the temperature to 200°C for 45 minutes then touch the start key to activate the airfryer. Halfway through cooking, flip the roast over.
5. When cooking is complete, transfer the roast to a plate. Cut into desired size slices and serve warm.

Beef Sausages

SERVES 4

| PREP TIME: 5 minutes | COOK TIME: 15 minutes	**4 (85 g) beef sausages**

1. Preheat the basket 1 with the grill plate inserted for three minutes by activating the automatic preheat key.
2. Place the beef sausages into basket 1 and set the temperature to 190°C for 15 minutes then touch the start key to activate the airfryer. Halfway through cooking, flip the beef sausages over.
3. When cooking is complete, transfer the beef sausages to a plate. Serve immediately.

Buttered Rib Eye Steak

SERVES 2

| PREP TIME: 20 minutes | COOK TIME: 18 minutes	**15 ml olive oil** **110 g unsalted butter, softened** **8 g fresh parsley, chopped** **2 (225 g) rib eye steaks** **2 tsps. garlic, minced** **5 ml Worcestershire sauce** **Salt and black pepper, to taste**

1. Mix the butter, garlic, parsley, Worcestershire sauce and salt in a small bowl.
2. Place the butter mixture onto a parchment paper, roll into a log and refrigerate for about 3 hours.
3. Rub the steaks generously with olive oil, salt and black pepper.
4. Preheat the basket 1 with the grill plate inserted for three minutes by activating the automatic preheat key.
5. Place the steaks into basket 1 and set the temperature to 200°C for 18 minutes then touch the start key to activate the airfryer. Halfway through cooking, flip the steaks over.
6. When cooking is complete, transfer the steaks to a plate and cut into desired size slices. Cut the butter log into slices and top over the steaks. Serve warm.

Veggie Stuffed Beef Rolls

SERVES 6

| PREP TIME: 20 minutes | COOK TIME: 16 minutes	**900 g beef flank steak, pounded to 3-mm thickness** **85 g roasted red bell peppers** **45 g fresh baby spinach** **6 Parmesan slices** **3 tbsps. prepared pesto** **Salt and black pepper, to taste**

1. Place the steak onto a smooth surface and spread evenly with the pesto.
2. Top with the cheese slices, roasted red peppers and spinach.
3. Roll up the steak tightly around the filling and secure with the toothpicks.
4. Preheat the basket 1 with the grill plate inserted for three minutes by activating the automatic preheat key.
5. Place the roll into basket 1 and set the temperature to 200°C for 16 minutes then touch the start key to activate the airfryer. Halfway through cooking, flip the roll over.
6. When cooking is complete, transfer the roll to a plate and serve warm.

Tasty Beef Jerky

SERVES 3

| PREP TIME: 20 minutes
| COOK TIME: 5 hours

450 g beef silverside, cut into thin strips
60 ml Worcestershire sauce
100 g dark brown sugar
120 ml soy sauce
15 ml chilli pepper sauce
1 tbsp. hickory liquid smoke
1 tsp. cayenne pepper
1 tsp. garlic powder
1 tsp. onion powder
½ tsp. smoked paprika
½ tsp. ground black pepper

1. Mix the brown sugar, all sauces, liquid smoke, and spices in a medium bowl.
2. Coat the beef strips with this marinade generously and marinate overnight.
3. Preheat the airfryer baskets with the grill plates inserted for three minutes by activating the automatic preheat key.
4. Carefully place half of beef strips in a single layer into each basket. Choose the basket 1 and select Dehydrate key, then set temperature to 70°C for 5 hours. Repeat with the basket 2 and touch the start key to activate.
5. When cooking is complete, transfer the beef jerky to a plate. Enjoy!

Beef and Vegetable Cubes

SERVES 4

| PREP TIME: 15 minutes
| COOK TIME: 18 minutes

30 ml olive oil
450 g top round steak, cut into cubes
115 g broccoli, cut into florets
115 g mushrooms, sliced
15 ml apple cider vinegar
1 tsp. shallot powder
1 tsp. fine sea salt
½ tsp. ground black pepper
¾ tsp. smoked cayenne pepper
½ tsp. garlic powder
¼ tsp. ground cumin
1 tsp. dried basil
1 tsp. celery seeds

1. Massage the olive oil, vinegar, salt, black pepper, shallot powder, garlic powder, cayenne pepper and cumin into the cubed steak, ensuring to coat each piece evenly. Let marinate for about 3 hours.
2. When ready to cook, remove the grill plate from basket 2 then preheat the airfryer baskets for three minutes by activating the automatic preheat key.
3. Place beef cubes onto the grill plate in basket 1 and set the temperature to 200°C for 14 minutes. Put the vegetables into basket 2 and set the temperature to 200°C for 18 minutes, then activate the Smart Finish key and touch the start key to activate the airfryer. Give both baskets a shake halfway through cooking.
4. When cooking is complete, serve the beef cubes hot with vegetables.

CHAPTER 6
Lamb

Spiced Lamb Satay

SERVES 2

| PREP TIME: 5 minutes
| COOK TIME: 10 minutes

Cooking spray
2 boneless lamb steaks
¼ tsp. cumin
1 tsp. ginger
½ tsp. nutmeg
Salt and ground black pepper, to taste

1. Combine the nutmeg, cumin, ginger, salt and pepper in a bowl.
2. Cube the lamb steaks and massage the spice mixture into each one.
3. Leave to marinate for about 10 minutes, then transfer onto metal skewers.
4. Preheat the basket 1 with the grill plate inserted for three minutes by activating the automatic preheat key.
5. Place the skewers into basket 1 and set the temperature to 200°C for 10 minutes then touch the start key to activate the airfryer. Halfway through cooking, flip the skewers over.
6. When cooking is complete, transfer the skewers to a plate and serve warm.

Lamb Chops with Herbs

SERVES 2

| PREP TIME: 10 minutes
| COOK TIME: 15 minutes

15 ml olive oil
4 (115 g) lamb chops
15 ml fresh lemon juice
1 tsp. dried thyme
1 tsp. dried rosemary
1 tsp. dried oregano
½ tsp. ground cumin
½ tsp. ground coriander
Salt and black pepper, to taste

1. Mix the oil, lemon juice, herbs, and spices in a large bowl.
2. Coat the lamb chops generously with the herb mixture and refrigerate to marinate for about 1 hour.
3. Preheat the basket 1 with the grill plate inserted for three minutes by activating the automatic preheat key.
4. Place the chops into basket 1 and set the temperature to 200°C for 15 minutes then touch the start key to activate the airfryer. Halfway through cooking, flip the lamb chops over.
5. When cooking is complete, transfer the chops to a plate. Serve hot.

Garlicky Lamb Chops

SERVES 2

| PREP TIME: 20 minutes
| COOK TIME: 17 minutes

3 g fresh oregano, chopped
4 g fresh thyme, chopped
8 (115 g) lamb chops
60 ml olive oil, divided
1 bulb garlic, halved
Salt and black pepper, to taste

1. Rub the garlic bulb halves with about 30 ml of the olive oil.
2. Mix the remaining olive oil, herbs, salt and black pepper in a large bowl. Coat the lamb chops with about 1 tbsp. of the herb mixture.
3. Preheat the airfryer baskets with the grill plates inserted for three minutes by activating the automatic preheat key.
4. Place 4 lamb chops and garlic bulb halve in a single layer into each basket. Select the Match Cook key and set basket 1 to 200°C for 17 minutes and touch the start key to activate. Halfway through cooking, flip the lamb chops over.
5. When cooking is complete, transfer the lamb chops to a plate and serve with herb mixture.

Herbed Leg of Lamb

SERVES 4

| PREP TIME: 10 minutes
| COOK TIME: 50 minutes

900 g leg of lamb
2 fresh rosemary sprigs
2 fresh thyme sprigs
30 ml olive oil
Salt and black pepper, to taste

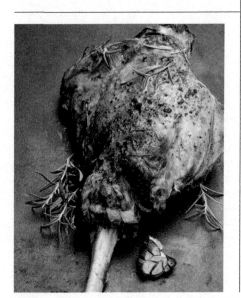

1. Season the leg of lamb with oil, salt and black pepper and wrap with the herb sprigs.
2. Preheat the basket 1 with the grill plate inserted for three minutes by activating the automatic preheat key.
3. Place leg of lamb into basket 1 and set the temperature to 200°C for 50 minutes then touch the start key to activate the airfryer. Halfway through cooking, flip the leg of lamb over.
4. When cooking is complete, transfer the leg of lamb to a plate. Serve hot.

34 | CHAPTER 6
| Lamb

Pesto Coated Rack of Lamb

SERVES 4

| PREP TIME: 15 minutes
| COOK TIME: 18 minutes

60 ml extra-virgin olive oil
1 (680 g) rack of lamb
½ bunch fresh mint
1 garlic clove
7 ml honey
Salt and black pepper, to taste

1. Put the oil, honey, mint, garlic, salt, and black pepper in a blender and pulse until smooth to make pesto.
2. Coat the rack of lamb with the pesto on both sides.
3. Preheat the basket 1 with the grill plate inserted for three minutes by activating the automatic preheat key.
4. Place the rack of lamb into basket 1 and set the temperature to 200°C for 18 minutes then touch the start key to activate the airfryer. Half-way through cooking, flip the rack of lamb over.
5. When cooking is complete, transfer the rack of lamb to a plate and cut the rack into individual chops to serve.

Lamb Ribs with Mint Yoghurt

SERVES 4

| PREP TIME: 5 minutes
| COOK TIME: 18 minutes

450 g lamb ribs
30 g mustard
1 tsp. rosemary, chopped
Salt and ground black pepper, to taste
240 ml Greek yoghurt
10 g mint leaves, chopped

1. Brush the lamb ribs with the mustard and season with rosemary, salt and black pepper.
2. Preheat the basket 1 with the grill plate inserted for three minutes by activating the automatic preheat key.
3. Place the lamb ribs into basket 1 and set the temperature to 200°C for 18 minutes then touch the start key to activate the airfryer. Half-way through cooking, flip the lamb ribs over.
4. Meanwhile, combine the mint leaves and yoghurt in a small bowl.
5. When cooking is complete, transfer the lamb ribs to a plate and serve with the mint yoghurt.

Lamb with Potatoes

SERVES 2

| PREP TIME: 20 minutes
| COOK TIME: 30 minutes

5 ml olive oil
225 g lamb meat
2 small potatoes, peeled and halved
½ small onion, peeled and halved
1 garlic clove, crushed
½ tbsp. dried rosemary, crushed

1. Rub the lamb meat evenly with garlic and rosemary.
2. Add the potatoes in a large bowl and stir in the olive oil and onion.
3. When ready to cook, remove the grill plate from basket 2 then preheat the airfryer baskets for three minutes by activating the automatic preheat key.
4. Place the lamb onto the grill plate in basket 1 and set the temperature to 190°C for 25 minutes. Put the vegetables into basket 2 and set the temperature to 200°C for 30 minutes, then activate the Smart Finish key and touch the start key to activate the airfryer. Halfway through cooking, flip the lamb and vegetables over.
5. When cooking is complete, serve the lamb hot with vegetables.

Mustard Lamb Loin Chops

SERVES 4

| PREP TIME: 15 minutes
| COOK TIME: 18 minutes

7 ml olive oil
8 (115 g) lamb loin chops
30 g Dijon mustard
15 ml fresh lemon juice
1 tsp. dried tarragon
Salt and black pepper, to taste

1. Mix the mustard, lemon juice, olive oil, tarragon, salt, and black pepper in a large bowl.
2. Coat the lamb chops generously with the mustard mixture.
3. Preheat the airfryer baskets with the grill plates inserted for three minutes by activating the automatic preheat key.
4. Place 4 chops in a single layer in each basket. Select the Match Cook key and set basket 1 to 200°C for 18 minutes and touch the start key to activate. Halfway through cooking, flip the lamb chops over.
5. When cooking is complete, transfer the lamb chops to a plate. Serve warm.

Greek Lamb Rib Rack

SERVES 5

| PREP TIME: 5 minutes
| COOK TIME: 14 minutes

30-60 ml olive oil
1 lamb rib rack (7 to 8 ribs)
60 ml freshly squeezed lemon juice
24 g minced garlic
2 tsps. minced fresh rosemary
1 tsp. oregano
1 tsp. minced fresh thyme
Salt and freshly ground black pepper, to taste

1. In a small mixing bowl, combine the lemon juice, rosemary, thyme, oregano, garlic, salt, pepper and olive oil and mix well.
2. Rub the herb mixture over the lamb, covering all the meat.
3. Preheat the basket 1 with the grill plate inserted for three minutes by activating the automatic preheat key.
4. Place the rack of lamb into basket 1 and set the temperature to 200°C for 14 minutes then touch the start key to activate the airfryer. Halfway through cooking, flip the rack of lamb over.
5. When cooking is complete, transfer the rack of lamb to a plate. Serve warm.

Spiced Lamb Steaks

SERVES 3

| PREP TIME: 15 minutes
| COOK TIME: 15 minutes

680 g boneless lamb sirloin steaks
½ onion, roughly chopped
5 garlic cloves, peeled
6 g fresh ginger, peeled
1 tsp. garam masala
1 tsp. ground fennel
½ tsp. cayenne pepper
½ tsp. ground cumin
½ tsp. ground cinnamon
Salt and black pepper, to taste

1. Put the onion, ginger, garlic, and spices in a blender and pulse until smooth.
2. Spread the lamb steaks with this mixture on both sides and refrigerate to marinate for about 24 hours.
3. Preheat the basket 1 with the grill plate inserted for three minutes by activating the automatic preheat key.
4. Place the lamb steaks into basket 1 and set the temperature to 200°C for 15 minutes then touch the start key to activate the airfryer. Halfway through cooking, flip the lamb steaks over.
5. When cooking is complete, transfer the lamb steaks to a plate. Serve warm.

Lamb Chops and Veggies

SERVES 4

| PREP TIME: 20 minutes
| COOK TIME: 18 minutes

45 ml olive oil
4 (170 g) lamb chops
2 carrots, peeled and cubed
1 parsnip, peeled and cubed
1 fennel bulb, cubed
1 garlic clove, minced
2 tbsps. dried rosemary
4 g fresh mint leaves, minced
Salt and black pepper, to taste

1. Mix the herbs, garlic and olive oil in a large bowl and coat the lamp chops generously with this mixture.
2. Marinate in the refrigerator for about 3 hours.
3. Soak the vegetables in a large pan of water for about 15 minutes.
4. When ready to cook, remove the grill plate from basket 2 then preheat the airfryer baskets for three minutes by activating the automatic preheat key.
5. Place the lamp chops onto the grill plate in basket 1 and set the temperature to 200°C for 18 minutes. Put the vegetables into basket 2 and set the temperature to 200°C for 16 minutes, then activate the Smart Finish key and touch the start key to activate the airfryer. Halfway through cooking, flip the lamp chops and vegetables over.
6. When cooking is complete, serve the lamp chops with vegetables.

CHAPTER 7
Poultry

Honey Glazed Chicken Drumsticks

SERVES 4

| PREP TIME: 15 minutes
| COOK TIME: 25 minutes

30 ml olive oil
4 (170 g) boneless chicken drumsticks
½ tbsp. fresh rosemary, minced
3 g fresh thyme, minced
60 ml Dijon mustard
15 ml honey
Salt and black pepper, to taste

1. Mix the mustard, honey, oil, herbs, salt and black pepper in a medium bowl.
2. Rub the chicken drumsticks with this marinade and refrigerate overnight.
3. Preheat the basket 1 with the grill plate inserted for three minutes by activating the automatic preheat key.
4. Place the drumsticks into basket 1 and set the temperature to 160°C for 25 minutes then touch the start key to activate the airfryer. Halfway through cooking, flip the drumsticks over.
5. When cooking is complete, transfer the drumsticks to a plate. Serve warm.

Spinach Stuffed Chicken Breasts

SERVES 2

| PREP TIME: 15 minutes
| COOK TIME: 29 minutes

15 ml olive oil
50 g fresh spinach
30 g ricotta cheese, shredded
2 (115 g) skinless, boneless chicken breasts
20 g cheddar cheese, grated
¼ tsp. paprika
Salt and ground black pepper, as required

1. Heat the olive oil in a medium frying pan over medium heat and cook the spinach for about 4 minutes.
2. Add the ricotta and cook for about 1 minute.
3. Cut the slits in each chicken breast horizontally and stuff with the spinach mixture.
4. Season each chicken breast evenly with salt and black pepper and top with cheddar cheese and paprika.
5. Preheat the basket 1 with the grill plate inserted for three minutes by activating the automatic preheat key.
6. Place the chicken breasts into basket 1 and set the temperature to 190°C for 25 minutes then touch the start key to activate the airfryer. Halfway through cooking, flip the chicken breasts over.
7. When cooking is complete, transfer the chicken breasts to a plate. Serve warm.

Appetising Chicken Thighs

SERVES 2

| PREP TIME: 15 minutes
| COOK TIME: 20 minutes

2 (115 g) skinless, boneless chicken thighs
1 scallion, finely chopped
50 g corn flour
1 garlic clove, minced
7 ml rice vinegar
7 ml soy sauce
5 g sugar
Salt and black pepper, as required

1. Mix all the ingredients except the chicken thighs and corn flour in a bowl.
2. Place the corn flour in another bowl.
3. Coat the chicken thighs into the marinade and then dredge into the corn flour.
4. Preheat the basket 1 with the grill plate inserted for three minutes by activating the automatic preheat key.
5. Place the chicken thighs into basket 1 and set the temperature to 200°C for 20 minutes then touch the start key to activate the airfryer. Halfway through cooking, flip the chicken thighs over.
6. When cooking is complete, transfer the chicken thighs to a plate. Serve warm.

Sweet and Salty Chicken Kebobs

SERVES 4

| PREP TIME: 20 minutes
| COOK TIME: 15 minutes

4 (115 g) skinless, boneless chicken thighs, cubed into 2.5 cm size
5 spring onions, cut into 2.5 cm pieces lengthwise
60 ml light soy sauce
15 ml mirin
5 g sugar
1 tsp. garlic salt
Wooden skewers, presoaked

1. Mix the soy sauce, mirin, garlic salt and sugar in a large baking dish.
2. Thread the spring onions and chicken onto pre-soaked wooden skewers.
3. Coat the skewers generously with this marinade.
4. Preheat the basket 1 with the grill plate inserted for three minutes by activating the automatic preheat key.
5. Place the skewers into basket 1 and set the temperature to 200°C for 15 minutes then touch the start key to activate the airfryer. Halfway through cooking, flip the skewers over.
6. When cooking is complete, transfer the skewers to a plate. Serve warm.

Crispy Chicken

SERVES 4

| **PREP TIME:** 10 minutes
| **COOK TIME:** 28 minutes

1 egg, beaten
60 g breadcrumbs
8 skinless, boneless chicken tenderloins
30 ml vegetable oil

1. Whisk the egg in a shallow dish and mix vegetable oil and breadcrumbs in another shallow dish.
2. Dip the chicken tenderloins in egg and then coat in the breadcrumb mixture.
3. Preheat the airfryer baskets with the grill plates inserted for three minutes by activating the automatic preheat key.
4. Place 4 chicken tenderloins in a single layer in each basket. Select the Match Cook key and set basket 1 to 200°C for 28 minutes and touch the start key to activate. Halfway through cooking, flip the chicken tenderloins over.
5. When cooking is complete, transfer the chicken tenderloins to a plate. Serve warm.

Buffalo Chicken Tenders

SERVES 3

| **PREP TIME:** 20 minutes
| **COOK TIME:** 24 minutes

450 g boneless, skinless chicken breasts, sliced into tenders
50 g pork rinds, crushed
60 g unflavoured whey protein powder
60 ml buffalo wing sauce
30 g butter, melted
15 ml water
1 large egg
½ tsp. garlic powder
Salt and ground black pepper, as required

1. Whisk the egg and water in a small bowl and coat the chicken with the egg mixture.
2. Mix the pork rinds, protein powder, garlic powder, salt and black pepper in another bowl.
3. Coat the chicken tenders with the pork rinds mixture.
4. Preheat the airfryer baskets with the grill plates inserted for three minutes by activating the automatic preheat key.
5. Place half of chicken tenders in a single layer in each basket. Select the Match Cook key and set basket 1 to 190°C for 24 minutes and touch the start key to activate. Halfway through cooking, flip the chicken tenders over.
6. When cooking is complete, transfer the chicken tenders to a plate. Top with the buffalo sauce to serve hot.

Surprisingly Tasty Chicken and Potato

SERVES 4

| PREP TIME: 10 minutes
| COOK TIME: 35 minutes

15 ml olive oil, scrubbed
Half of whole chicken (about 1 kg)
450 g small potatoes
Salt and black pepper, to taste

1. Season the chicken with salt and black pepper to taste.
2. Mix the potatoes, oil, salt and black pepper in a bowl and toss to coat well.
3. When ready to cook, remove the grill plate from basket 2 then preheat the airfryer baskets for three minutes by activating the automatic preheat key.
4. Place the chicken onto the grill plate in basket 1 and set the temperature to 200°C for 35 minutes. Put the potatoes into basket 2 and set the temperature to 200°C for 30 minutes, then activate the Smart Finish key and touch the start key to activate the airfryer. Halfway through cooking, flip the chicken and potatoes over.
5. When cooking is complete, serve the chicken with potatoes.

Juicy Herbed Drumsticks

SERVES 4

| PREP TIME: 10 minutes
| COOK TIME: 22 minutes

1 g fresh rosemary, minced
30 ml olive oil
2 g fresh thyme, minced
4 boneless chicken drumsticks
60 ml Dijon mustard
15 ml honey
Salt and freshly ground black pepper, to taste

1. Mix all the ingredients in a bowl except the drumsticks until well combined.
2. Stir in the drumsticks and coat generously with the mixture.
3. Cover and refrigerate to marinate overnight.
4. Preheat the basket 1 with the grill plate inserted for three minutes by activating the automatic preheat key.
5. Place drumsticks into basket 1 and set the temperature to 200°C for 22 minutes then touch the start key to activate the airfryer. Halfway through cooking, flip the drumsticks over.
6. When cooking is complete, transfer the drumsticks to a plate. Serve warm.

Chicken with Apple

SERVES 8

| PREP TIME: 10 minutes
| COOK TIME: 20 minutes

2 (115 g) boneless, skinless chicken thighs, sliced into chunks
1 large apple, cored and cubed
120 ml apple cider
30 ml maple syrup
6 g fresh ginger, finely grated
1 shallot, thinly sliced
1 tsp. fresh thyme, minced
Salt and black pepper, as required

1. Mix the shallot, ginger, thyme, apple cider, maple syrup, salt and black pepper in a bowl.
2. Coat the chicken thighs generously with the marinade and refrigerate to marinate for about 8 hours.
3. When ready to cook, remove the grill plate from basket 2 then preheat the airfryer baskets for three minutes by activating the automatic preheat key.
4. Place the chicken pieces onto the grill plate in basket 1 and set the temperature to 200°C for 20 minutes. Put the apples into basket 2 and set the temperature to 200°C for 15 minutes, then activate the Smart Finish key and touch the start key to activate the airfryer. Give both baskets a shake halfway through cooking.
5. When cooking is complete, serve the chicken hot with apples.

Bacon Wrapped Chicken Breasts

SERVES 4

| PREP TIME: 20 minutes
| COOK TIME: 28 minutes

2 (225 g) chicken breasts, cut each breast in half horizontally
12 rashers of bacon
7 ml honey
6-7 Fresh basil leaves
30 ml water
30 ml fish sauce
15 g palm sugar
Salt and ground black pepper, as required

1. Cook the palm sugar in a small heavy-bottomed pan over medium-low heat for about 3 minutes until caramelised.
2. Stir in the basil, fish sauce and water and dish out in a small bowl.
3. Season each chicken breast with salt and black pepper to taste and coat with the palm sugar mixture.
4. Refrigerate to marinate for about 6 hours and wrap each chicken piece with 3 rashers of bacon. Dip into the honey.
5. Preheat the basket 1 with the grill plate inserted for three minutes by activating the automatic preheat key.
6. Place the chicken breasts into basket 1 and set the temperature to 200°C for 25 minutes then touch the start key to activate the airfryer. Halfway through cooking, flip the chicken breasts over.
7. When cooking is complete, transfer the chicken breasts to a plate. Serve warm.

Mini Turkey Meatloaves with Carrot

SERVES 4

| PREP TIME: 6 minutes
| COOK TIME: 22 minutes

10 ml olive oil
340 g turkey breast, minced
1 egg white
50 g minced onion
30 g grated carrot
2 garlic cloves, minced
20 g ground almonds
1 tsp. dried marjoram

1. In a medium bowl, stir together the onion, carrot, garlic, almonds, olive oil, marjoram and egg white.
2. Fold in the minced turkey. With your hands, gently but thoroughly mix until well combined.
3. Double 16 foil muffin cup liners to make 8 cups. Divide the turkey mixture evenly among the liners.
4. When ready to cook, remove the grill plates and preheat the airfryer baskets for three minutes by activating the automatic preheat key.
5. Place 4 cups in a single layer in each basket. Select the Match Cook key then set basket 1 to 200°C for 22 minutes, then touch the start key to activate the airfryer.
6. When cooking is complete, transfer the turkey meatloaves to a plate. Serve warm.

Glazed Chicken Wings

SERVES 4

| PREP TIME: 10 minutes
| COOK TIME: 25 minutes

8 chicken wings
16 g plain flour
1 tsp. garlic, chopped finely
15 ml fresh lemon juice
15 ml soy sauce
½ tsp. dried oregano, crushed
Salt and freshly ground black pepper, to taste

1. Mix all the ingredients except the chicken wings and flour in a large bowl.
2. Coat the wings generously with the marinade and refrigerate for about 2 hours.
3. Remove the chicken wings from the marinade and coat with the flour evenly.
4. Preheat the basket 1 with the grill plate inserted for three minutes by activating the automatic preheat key.
5. Place the chicken wings into basket 1 and set the temperature to 200°C for 25 minutes then touch the start key to activate the airfryer. Halfway through cooking, flip the chicken wings over.
6. When cooking is complete, transfer the chicken wings to a plate. Serve hot.

CHAPTER 8

Fish and Seafood

Roasted Cod with Broccoli

SERVES 2

| PREP TIME: 5 minutes
| COOK TIME: 15 minutes

2 (170 g) fresh cod fillets
15 ml reduced-sodium soy sauce
10 ml honey
400 g fresh broccoli florets
30 g butter, melted
2 g sesame seeds
Salt and black pepper, to taste

1. In a small bowl, combine the soy sauce and honey and mix well.
2. Brush the cod fillets with the soy mixture and sprinkle with sesame seeds.
3. Mix the broccoli, butter, salt, and black pepper in a bowl and toss to coat well.
4. When ready to cook, remove the grill plate from basket 2 then preheat the airfryer baskets for three minutes by activating the automatic preheat key.
5. Place the cod fillets onto the grill plate in basket 1 and set the temperature to 200°C for 14 minutes. Put the broccoli into basket 2 and set the temperature to 200°C for 20 minutes, then activate the Smart Finish key and touch the start key to activate the airfryer.
6. When cooking is complete, serve the cod fillets with broccoli florets.

Salmon with Dill Sauce

SERVES 5

| PREP TIME: 15 minutes
| COOK TIME: 10 minutes

10 ml olive oil
2 (170 g) salmon fillets
120 ml Greek yoghurt
6 g fresh dill, chopped and divided
60 g sour cream
Salt, to taste

1. Coat the salmon fillets with olive oil and season with a pinch of salt.
2. Preheat the basket 1 with the grill plate inserted for three minutes by activating the automatic preheat key.
3. Place the salmon into basket 1 and set the temperature to 200°C for 10 minutes then touch the start key to activate the airfryer. Halfway through cooking, flip the salmon fillets over.
4. Meanwhile, mix the remaining ingredients in a bowl to make dill sauce.
5. When cooking is complete, transfer the salmon fillets to a plate. Serve the salmon with dill sauce.

Orange Prawns

SERVES 4

| PREP TIME: 20 minutes
| COOK TIME: 10 minutes

Cooking spray
80 ml orange juice
450 g medium prawns, peeled and deveined, with tails off
3 tsps. minced garlic
1 tsp. Old Bay seasoning
¼ to ½ tsp. cayenne pepper

1. In a medium bowl, combine the orange juice, Old Bay seasoning, garlic and cayenne pepper.
2. Dry the prawns with paper towels to remove excess water.
3. Add the prawns to the marinade and stir to coat well. Cover with clingfilm and place in the refrigerator for about 30 minutes so the prawns can soak up the marinade.
4. When ready to cook, remove the grill plate from basket 1 then preheat the airfryer basket for three minutes by activating the automatic preheat key.
5. Put the prawns into basket 1 and spray lightly with cooking spray. Set the temperature to 200°C for 10 minutes, then touch the start key to activate the airfryer. Halfway through cooking, give the prawns a shake.
6. When cooking is complete, transfer the prawns to a plate. Serve warm.

Juicy Salmon and Asparagus

SERVES 2

| PREP TIME: 5 minutes
| COOK TIME: 18 minutes

5 ml olive oil
2 salmon fillets
4 asparagus stalks
60 ml champagne
60 ml white sauce
Salt and black pepper, to taste

1. Mix all the ingredients in a medium bowl.
2. When ready to cook, remove the grill plate from basket 2 then preheat the airfryer baskets for three minutes by activating the automatic preheat key.
3. Place the salmon fillets onto the grill plate in basket 1 and set the temperature to 200°C for 15 minutes. Put the asparagus stalks into basket 2 and set the temperature to 200°C for 18 minutes, then activate the Smart Finish key and touch the start key to activate the airfryer. Halfway through cooking, flip the salmon and asparagus over.
4. When cooking is complete, serve the salmon with asparagus.

Cod Cakes with Salad Greens

SERVES 4

| PREP TIME: 15 minutes
| COOK TIME: 15 minutes

Cooking spray
450 g cod fillets, cut into chunks
1 large egg, beaten
60 g panko bread crumbs
10 g packed fresh basil leaves
3 cloves garlic, crushed
½ tsp. smoked paprika
¼ tsp. salt
¼ tsp. pepper
Salad greens, for serving

1. In a food processor, pulse the cod, garlic, basil, smoked paprika, salt and pepper until the cod is finely chopped, stirring occasionally.
2. Form this mixture into 8 patties, about 5-cm in diameter. Dip each first into the egg, then into the panko, patting to adhere. Spray with cooking spray on one side.
3. Preheat the airfryer baskets with the grill plates inserted for three minutes by activating the automatic preheat key.
4. Carefully place 4 cod cakes in a single layer into each basket, oil-side down; spray with cooking spray. Select the Match Cook key and set basket 1 to 200°C for 15 minutes and touch the start key to activate. Halfway through cooking, flip the cod cakes over.
5. When cooking is complete, transfer the cod cakes to a plate. Serve with salad greens.

Simple Salmon Bites

SERVES 4

| PREP TIME: 15 minutes
| COOK TIME: 15 minutes

Cooking spray
4 (140 g) tins pink salmon, skinless, boneless in water, drained
2 eggs, beaten
100 g whole-wheat panko bread crumbs
60 g finely minced red bell pepper
2 tbsps. parsley flakes
2 tsps. Old Bay seasoning

1. In a medium bowl, mix the salmon, eggs, red bell pepper, panko bread crumbs, parsley flakes, and Old Bay seasoning.
2. Using a small cookie scoop, form the salmon mixture into 20 balls.
3. Preheat the airfryer baskets with the grill plates inserted for three minutes by activating the automatic preheat key.
4. Place half of salmon bites in a single layer in each basket and spray lightly with cooking spray. Select the Match Cook key and set basket 1 to 200°C for 15 minutes and touch the start key to activate.
5. Halfway through cooking, flip the salmon bites over and lightly spray with cooking spray.
6. When cooking is complete, transfer the salmon bites to a plate. Serve warm.

Chilli Cod Sticks

SERVES 2

PREP TIME: 20 minutes COOK TIME: 10 minutes	3 (115 g) skinless cod fillets, cut into rectangular pieces 4 eggs 95 g flour 1 green chilli, finely chopped 2 garlic cloves, minced 10 ml light soy sauce Salt and ground black pepper, to taste

1. Place the flour in a shallow dish and whisk the eggs, garlic, green chilli, soy sauce, salt and pepper in a second dish.
2. Coat the cod evenly in flour, then dip in the egg mixture.
3. Preheat the basket 1 with the grill plate inserted for three minutes by activating the automatic preheat key.
4. Place the cod pieces into basket 1 and set the temperature to 200°C for 10 minutes then touch the start key to activate the airfryer. Halfway through cooking, flip the cod pieces over.
5. When cooking is complete, transfer the cod pieces to a plate. Serve warm.

Cajun Spiced Salmon

SERVES 2

PREP TIME: 10 minutes COOK TIME: 12 minutes	2 (200 g) (2-cm thick) salmon fillets 1 tbsp. Cajun seasoning 15 ml fresh lemon juice 2 g coconut sugar

1. Season the salmon fillets evenly with Cajun seasoning and coconut sugar.
2. Preheat the basket 1 with the grill plate inserted for three minutes by activating the automatic preheat key.
3. Place the salmon fillets into basket 1 and set the temperature to 200°C for 12 minutes then touch the start key to activate the airfryer. Halfway through cooking, flip the salmon over.
4. When cooking is complete, transfer the salmon fillets to a plate. Drizzle with the lemon juice and serve hot.

Mahi Mahi with Green Beans

SERVES 4

PREP TIME: 15 minutes COOK TIME: 15 minutes	15 ml olive oil 4 (170 g) Mahi Mahi fillets 500 g green beans 2 tbsps. fresh dill, chopped 15 ml avocado oil 2 garlic cloves, minced 30 ml fresh lemon juice Salt, as required

1. Combine the dill, garlic, lemon juice, salt and olive oil in a small bowl. Coat the Mahi Mahi in this garlic mixture.
2. Mix the green beans, avocado oil and salt in a large bowl.
3. Preheat the airfryer baskets with the grill plates inserted for three minutes by activating the automatic preheat key.
4. Carefully place the Mahi Mahi into basket 1 and arrange the green beans into the basket 2. Select the Match Cook key and set basket 1 to 200°C for 15 minutes and touch the start key to activate. Halfway through cooking, flip the Mahi Mahi over and give the green beans a shake.
5. When cooking is complete, serve Mahi Mahi immediately with green beans.

Easy Cod with Paprika

SERVES 2

| PREP TIME: 10 minutes **| COOK TIME:** 12 minutes	**10 ml olive oil** **2 (170 g) (4-cm thick) cod fillets** **1 tsp. smoked paprika** **1 tsp. cayenne pepper** **1 tsp. onion powder** **1 tsp. garlic powder** **Salt and ground black pepper, as required**

1. Drizzle the cod fillets with olive oil and rub with all the spices.
2. Preheat the basket 1 with the grill plate inserted for three minutes by activating the automatic preheat key.
3. Place the cod fillets into basket 1 and set the temperature to 200°C for 12 minutes then touch the start key to activate the airfryer. Halfway through cooking, flip the cod fillets over.
4. When cooking is complete, transfer the cod fillets to a plate. Serve warm.

Sesame Seeds Coated Tuna with Spinach

SERVES 2

| PREP TIME: 15 minutes **| COOK TIME:** 15 minutes	**2 (170 g) tuna steaks** **40 g white sesame seeds** **10 g black sesame seeds** **1 egg white** **1 small onion, chopped** **30 ml olive oil** **150 g fresh spinach** **1 tsp. ginger, minced** **Salt and black pepper, to taste**

1. Whisk the egg white in a shallow bowl.
2. Mix the sesame seeds, salt and pepper in another bowl.
3. Dip the tuna steaks into the whisked egg white and dredge into the sesame seeds mixture.
4. Put the olive oil, onion and ginger in a medium bowl.
5. When ready to cook, remove the grill plate from basket 2 then preheat the airfryer baskets for three minutes by activating the automatic preheat key.
6. Place the tuna steaks onto the grill plate in basket 1 and set the temperature to 200°C for 15 minutes. Put the onion into basket 2 and set the temperature to 200°C for 12 minutes, then activate the Smart Finish key and touch the start key to activate the airfryer.
7. With 6 minutes remaining, flip the tuna steaks over. Add spinach, salt, and black pepper in the basket. Continue to cook for 6 minutes.
8. When cooking is complete, serve the tuna steaks with vegetables.

CHAPTER 9
Snack

Buffalo Cauliflower with Sour Dip

SERVES 6

| PREP TIME: 10 minutes
| COOK TIME: 20 minutes

15 ml olive oil
1 large head cauliflower, separated into small florets
½ tsp. garlic powder
80 ml low-sodium hot wing sauce, divided
160 ml nonfat Greek yoghurt
1 celery stalk, chopped
10 g crumbled blue stilton cheese
½ tsp. Tabasco sauce

1. In a large bowl, toss the cauliflower florets with the oil. Sprinkle with the garlic powder and toss again to coat well.
2. When ready to cook, remove the grill plates and preheat the airfryer baskets for three minutes by activating the automatic preheat key.
3. Place half of the cauliflower in each basket. Select the Match Cook key then set basket 1 to 200°C for 20 minutes, then touch the start key to activate the airfryer.
4. Halfway through cooking, give the cauliflower a shake.
5. When cooking is complete, transfer the cauliflower to a serving bowl and and toss with the hot wing sauce.
6. In a small bowl, stir together the yoghurt, celery, Tabasco sauce, and blue stilton cheese. Serve the cauliflower with the dip.

Roasted Cashews with Rosemary

SERVES 4

| PREP TIME: 5 minutes
| COOK TIME: 5 minutes

Cooking spray
2 sprigs of fresh rosemary (1 chopped and 1 whole)
5 ml olive oil
320 g roasted and unsalted whole cashews
2 ml honey
1 tsp. coarse salt

1. In a medium bowl, whisk together the olive oil, chopped rosemary, coarse salt, and honey. Set aside.
2. When ready to cook, remove the grill plate from basket 1 then pre-heat the airfryer basket for three minutes by activating the automatic preheat key.
3. Place the cashews and the whole rosemary sprig into basket 1 and spray with cooking spray. Set the temperature to 150°C for 5 minutes, then touch the start key to activate the airfryer. Halfway through cooking, give the cashews a shake.
4. When cooking is complete, discard the rosemary and transfer the cashews to the olive oil mixture, tossing to coat well.
5. Allow to cool for 15 minutes before serving.

Spicy Kale Crisps

SERVES 4

| PREP TIME: 5 minutes
| COOK TIME: 15 minutes

Cooking spray
500 g kale, large stems removed and chopped
10 g rapeseed oil
¼ tsp. coarse salt
¼ tsp. smoked paprika

1. In a large bowl, toss the kale, oil, smoked paprika and coarse salt.
2. When ready to cook, remove the grill plates and preheat the airfryer baskets for three minutes by activating the automatic preheat key.
3. Place half the kale in each basket and spray with cooking spray. Select the Match Cook key then set basket 1 to 150°C for 15 minutes, then touch the start key to activate the airfryer. Give both baskets a shake halfway through cooking.
4. When cooking is complete, transfer the kale to a plate and allow to cool on a wire rack for 3 to 5 minutes before serving.

Crispy Spiced Chickpeas

SERVES 4

| PREP TIME: 5 minutes
| COOK TIME: 10 minutes

15 ml olive oil
1 tin (425 g) chickpeas, rinsed and dried with paper towels
½ tsp. dried rosemary
½ tsp. dried chives
½ tsp. dried parsley
¼ tsp. sweet paprika
¼ tsp. cayenne pepper
¼ tsp. mustard powder
Coarse salt and freshly ground black pepper, to taste

1. In a large bowl, combine all the ingredients, except for the coarse salt and black pepper, and toss to coat well.
2. When ready to cook, remove the grill plate from basket 1 then preheat the airfryer basket for three minutes by activating the automatic preheat key.
3. Scrape the chickpeas and seasonings into basket 1 and set the temperature to 180°C for 10 minutes, then touch the start key to activate the airfryer. Halfway through cooking, give the chickpeas a shake.
4. When cooking is complete, transfer the chickpeas to a bowl. Sprinkle with coarse salt and black pepper and serve hot.

Homemade Croutons

SERVES 4

| PREP TIME: 5 minutes
| COOK TIME: 10 minutes

15 ml olive oil
2 slices friendly bread
Hot soup, for serving

1. Cut the slices of bread into medium-size chunks.
2. When ready to cook, remove the grill plate from basket 1 then pre-heat the airfryer basket for three minutes by activating the automatic preheat key.
3. Brush the basket 1 with the olive oil and place the bread chunks. Set the temperature to 200°C for 10 minutes, then touch the start key to activate the airfryer. Halfway through cooking, give the bread chunks a shake.
4. When cooking is complete, transfer the bread chunks to a plate. Serve with hot soup.

Herbed Pitta Crisps

SERVES 4

| PREP TIME: 5 minutes
| COOK TIME: 6 minutes

Cooking spray
2 whole grain 15-cm pittas
¼ tsp. dried basil
¼ tsp. garlic powder
¼ tsp. marjoram
¼ tsp. ground oregano
¼ tsp. ground thyme
¼ tsp. salt

1. Mix all the seasonings together in a small bowl.
2. Cut each pitta half into 4 wedges. Break apart wedges at the fold.
3. Mist one side of pitta wedges with oil. Sprinkle with half of seasoning mix.
4. Turn the pitta wedges over, mist the other side with oil, and sprinkle with remaining seasonings.
5. When ready to cook, remove the grill plate from basket 1 then pre-heat the airfryer basket for three minutes by activating the automatic preheat key.
6. Put the pitta wedges into basket 1 and set the temperature to 160°C for 6 minutes, then touch the start key to activate the airfryer, shaking every 2 minutes.
7. When cooking is complete, transfer the pitta wedges to a plate and serve hot.

Crispy Green Olives

SERVES 4

| PREP TIME: 5 minutes | COOK TIME: 8 minutes	Cooking spray 50 g bread crumbs 1 (160 g) jar pitted green olives 1 egg 50 g plain flour Salt and pepper, to taste

1. Remove the green olives from the jar and dry thoroughly with paper towels.
2. In a small bowl, combine the flour with salt and black pepper to taste. Place the bread crumbs in another small bowl. In a third small bowl, beat the egg.
3. Dip the olives in the flour, then the egg, and then the bread crumbs.
4. When ready to cook, remove the grill plate from basket 1 then preheat the airfryer basket for three minutes by activating the automatic preheat key.
5. Spray the breaded olives with cooking spray and put into basket 1 and set the temperature to 200°C for 8 minutes, then touch the start key to activate the airfryer. Halfway through cooking, carefully turn the breaded olives over.
6. When cooking is complete, transfer the breaded olives to a plate. Cool before serving.

Garlic Matchstick Fries

SERVES 2

| PREP TIME: 5 minutes | COOK TIME: 18 minutes	15 ml vegetable oil 1 large russet potato (about 340 g), scrubbed clean, and julienned Leaves from 1 sprig fresh rosemary 1 garlic clove, thinly sliced Coarse salt and freshly ground black pepper, to taste Flaky sea salt, for serving

1. Place the julienned potatoes in a large colander and rinse under cold running water until the water runs clear. Spread the potatoes out on a double-thick layer of paper towels and pat dry.
2. In a large bowl, combine the potatoes, vegetable oil, and rosemary. Season with coarse salt and pepper to taste and toss to coat evenly.
3. When ready to cook, remove the grill plate from basket 1 then preheat the airfryer basket for three minutes by activating the automatic preheat key.
4. Put the potatoes into basket 1 and set the temperature to 200°C for 18 minutes, then touch the start key to activate the airfryer. Halfway through cooking, give the fries a shake and add the garlic.
5. When cooking is complete, transfer the fries to a plate and sprinkle with flaky sea salt while they're hot. Serve immediately.

Healthy Courgette and Potato Tots

SERVES 4

| PREP TIME: 5 minutes | COOK TIME: 14 minutes	Cooking spray 30 g shredded Cheddar cheese 1 large courgette, grated 1 large egg, beaten 1 medium baked potato, skin ½ tsp. coarse salt removed and mashed

1. Wrap the grated courgette in a paper towel and squeeze out any excess liquid, then combine the courgette, baked potato, cheese, egg, and coarse salt in a large bowl.
2. Shape this mixture into several small tots.
3. When ready to cook, remove the grill plates and preheat the airfryer baskets for three minutes by activating the automatic preheat key.
4. Place half of tots in each basket and spray with cooking spray. Select the Match Cook key then set basket 1 to 200°C for 14 minutes, then touch the start key to activate the airfryer.
5. For even browning, carefully turn the tots over halfway through cooking using a silicone spatula.
6. When cooking is complete, transfer the tots to a plate and allow to cool on a wire rack for 5 minutes before serving.

Spicy Chicken Bites with Courgette Chips

SERVES 4

| PREP TIME: 10 minutes
| COOK TIME: 20 minutes

Cooking spray
225 g boneless and skinless chicken thighs, cut into 30 pieces
30 ml hot sauce
¼ tsp. coarse salt
1 courgette, cut into 3-mm-thick slices
1 tsp. Cajun seasoning

1. Season the chicken bites with the coarse salt in a medium bowl.
2. Mix the courgette slices and Cajun seasoning in another bowl.
3. When ready to cook, remove the grill plate from basket 2 then preheat the airfryer baskets for three minutes by activating the automatic preheat key.
4. Place the chicken bites onto the grill plate in basket 1 and spray lightly with cooking spray. Set the temperature to 200°C for 15 minutes. Put the courgette slices into basket 2 and spray with cooking spray. Set the temperature to 200°C for 20 minutes, then activate the Smart Finish key and touch the start key to activate the airfryer. Give both baskets a shake halfway through cooking.
5. Meanwhile, pour the hot sauce into a large bowl.
6. When cooking is complete, transfer the bites and courgette slices to a plate. Add the bites to the sauce bowl, tossing to coat well. Serve warm with courgette slices.

Coconut-Crusted Prawn

SERVES 2-4

| PREP TIME: 10 minutes
| COOK TIME: 7 minutes

Cooking spray
225 g medium prawns, peeled and deveined (tails intact)
240 ml tinned coconut milk
50 g panko bread crumbs
50 g unsweetened desiccated coconut
Finely grated zest of 1 lime
Coarse salt, to taste
Freshly ground black pepper, to taste
240 ml coconut yoghurt
1 small or ½ medium cucumber, halved and deseeded
1 jalapeno pepper, deseeded and minced

1. In a bowl, combine the prawns, coconut milk, lime zest and ½ tsp. coarse salt. Let the prawns stand for about 10 minutes.
2. Meanwhile, in a separate bowl, stir together the bread crumbs and desiccated coconut and season with salt and pepper to taste.
3. A few at a time, add the prawns to the bread crumb mixture and toss to coat evenly. Transfer the prawns to a wire rack set over a baking sheet. Spray the prawns all over with cooking spray.
4. When ready to cook, remove the grill plate from basket 1 then preheat the airfryer basket for three minutes by activating the automatic preheat key.
5. Put the prawns into basket 1 and set the temperature to 200°C for 7 minutes, then touch the start key to activate the airfryer. Halfway through cooking, give the prawns a shake.
6. When cooking is complete, transfer the prawns to a serving platter and season with more salt.
7. Grate the cucumber into a small bowl. Stir in the coconut yoghurt and jalapeno pepper and season with salt and pepper. Serve alongside the prawns while they're warm.

CHAPTER 10
Dessert

Classic Buttermilk Scones

SERVES 4

| PREP TIME: 15 minutes
| COOK TIME: 8 minutes

Butter for brushing
210 g plain flour
180 ml buttermilk
75 g unsalted butter, cut into cubes
4 g granulated sugar
4 g baking soda
3 g baking powder
Salt, to taste

1. Grease a 13-cm pie dish lightly.
2. Sift together flour, baking soda, baking powder, sugar and salt in a large bowl.
3. Add the cold butter and mix until a coarse crumb is formed.
4. Stir in the buttermilk gently and mix until a dough is formed.
5. Press the dough into 1-cm thickness onto a floured surface and cut out circles with a 4-cm round cookie cutter.
6. Arrange the scones in the pie dish in a single layer and brush with the butter.
7. When ready to cook, remove the grill plate from basket 1 then pre-heat the airfryer basket for three minutes by activating the automatic preheat key.
8. Put the pie dish into basket 1 and set the temperature to 200°C for 8 minutes, then touch the start key to activate the airfryer, until golden brown.
9. When cooking is complete, serve warm.

Strawberry Cupcakes

SERVES 8

| PREP TIME: 10 minutes
| COOK TIME: 10 minutes

For the Cupcakes:
110 g self-rising flour
100 g caster sugar
100 g butter
2 eggs
½ tsp. vanilla essence
For the Icing:
125 g icing sugar
50 g butter
50 g fresh strawberries, blended
15 ml whipped cream
½ tsp. pink food colour

1. Grease 8 muffin tins lightly.
2. Mix all the cupcakes ingredients in a large bowl until well combined. Transfer the mixture into muffin tins.
3. When ready to cook, remove the grill plates and preheat the airfryer baskets for three minutes by activating the automatic preheat key.
4. Place 4 muffin tins in each basket. Select the Match Cook key then set basket 1 to 170°C for 10 minutes, then touch the start key to activate the airfryer. Bake until toothpick inserted in centre comes out clean.
5. When cooking is complete, transfer the muffin tins to a plate.
6. Mix all the icing ingredients in a large bowl until well combined.
7. Fill the pastry bag with icing and top each cupcake evenly with frosting to serve.

Simple Sunflower Seeds Bread

SERVES 4

| PREP TIME: 15 minutes
| COOK TIME: 18 minutes

240 ml lukewarm water
85 g whole wheat flour
85 g plain flour
45 g sunflower seeds
½ sachet instant yeast
1 tsp. salt

1. Grease a 18 x 10 cm cake pan.
2. Mix together the flours, sunflower seeds, yeast and salt in a bowl.
3. Add the water gently and knead for about 5 minutes until a dough is formed.
4. Cover the dough with a clingfilm and keep in warm place for about half an hour.
5. Arrange the dough into the cake pan.
6. When ready to cook, remove the grill plate from basket 1 then preheat the airfryer basket for three minutes by activating the automatic preheat key.
7. Place the cake pan into basket 1 and set the temperature to 200°C for 18 minutes, then touch the start key to activate the airfryer. Bake until toothpick inserted in centre comes out clean.
8. When cooking is complete, remove the bread from the airfryer. Cut into desired slices and serve warm.

Apple Tart

SERVES 2

| PREP TIME: 15 minutes
| COOK TIME: 25 minutes

70 g butter, chopped and divided
1 large apple, peeled, cored and cut into 12 wedges
100 g flour
1 egg yolk
30 g sugar

1. Grease a 18x13 cm baking pan lightly.
2. Mix half of the butter and flour in a small bowl until a soft dough is formed.
3. Roll the dough into 15-cm round on a floured surface.
4. Place the remaining butter and sugar into the baking pan and arrange the apple wedges in a circular pattern.
5. Top with rolled dough and press gently along the edges of the baking pan.
6. When ready to cook, remove the grill plate from basket 1 then preheat the airfryer basket for three minutes by activating the automatic preheat key.
7. Place the baking pan into basket 1 and set the temperature to 200°C for 25 minutes, then touch the start key to activate the airfryer.
8. When cooking is complete, let the apple tart cool for 5-10 minutes and serve warm.

Vanilla Pecan Pie

SERVES 6

| PREP TIME: 10 minutes
| COOK TIME: 30 minutes

75 g butter, melted
2 large eggs
150 g brown sugar
50 g caster sugar
100 g pecan halves
1 frozen pie crust, thawed
14 g flour
1 tsp. vanilla extract

1. Grease a 13-cm pie dish lightly.
2. Mix both sugars, eggs and butter in a medium bowl until smooth.
3. Stir in the flour, milk and vanilla extract and beat until well combined. Fold in the pecan halves.
4. Arrange the crust in the bottom of pie dish. Put the pecan mixture in pie crust evenly.
5. When ready to cook, remove the grill plate from basket 1 then preheat the airfryer basket for three minutes by activating the automatic preheat key.
6. Put the pie dish into basket 1 and set the temperature to 150°C for 30 minutes, then touch the start key to activate the airfryer.
7. When cooking is complete, let the pecan pie cool for 10 minutes and serve warm.

Homemade Shortbread Fingers

SERVES 10

| PREP TIME: 10 minutes
| COOK TIME: 14 minutes

cooking spray
170 g butter
200 g plain flour
60 g caster sugar

1. Mix the sugar, flour and butter in a medium bowl to form a dough.
2. Cut the dough into 10 equal sized fingers and prick the fingers lightly with a fork. Spray the fingers with cooking spray.
3. When ready to cook, remove the grill plates and preheat the airfryer baskets for three minutes by activating the automatic preheat key.
4. Place 5 fingers in a single layer in each basket. Select the Match Cook key then set basket 1 to 180°C for 14 minutes, then touch the start key to activate the airfryer.
5. When cooking is complete, dish out and serve warm.

Heavenly Tasty Lava Cake

SERVES 4

| PREP TIME: 10 minutes
| COOK TIME: 6 minutes

150 g unsalted butter	65 g sugar
160 g chocolate chips, melted	45 g fresh raspberries
2 eggs	Salt, to taste
80 g plain flour	

1. Grease four 7-cm ramekins lightly.
2. Mix the sugar, butter, eggs, chocolate mixture, flour and salt in a bowl until well combined.
3. Fold in the melted chocolate chips and divide this mixture into the prepared ramekins.
4. When ready to cook, remove the grill plates and preheat the airfryer baskets for three minutes by activating the automatic preheat key.
5. Place 2 ramekins in each basket. Select the Match Cook key then set basket 1 to 180°C for 6 minutes, then touch the start key to activate the airfryer. Bake until toothpick inserted in centre comes out clean.
6. When cooking is complete, garnish with raspberries and serve immediately.

Nuts Stuffed Apples

SERVES 4

| PREP TIME: 10 minutes
| COOK TIME: 13 minutes

4 small firm apples, cored	80 g golden sultanas
120 ml whipped cream	65 g blanched almonds
60 g sugar, divided	½ tsp. vanilla extract

1. Grease a 18x13 cm baking dish lightly.
2. Put the almonds, sultanas and half of sugar in a food processor and pulse until chopped.
3. Stuff the sultana mixture inside each apple and arrange the apples in the prepared baking dish.
4. When ready to cook, remove the grill plate from basket 1 then preheat the airfryer basket for three minutes by activating the automatic preheat key.
5. Place the baking dish into basket 1 and set the temperature to 180°C for 10 minutes, then touch the start key to activate the airfryer.
6. When cooking is complete, set the apples aside to let cool.
7. Put the cream, remaining sugar and vanilla extract on medium heat in a pan and cook for about 3 minutes, continuously stirring.
8. Turn off the heat and serve apple with vanilla sauce.

Decadent Cheesecake

SERVES 6

| PREP TIME: 15 minutes
| COOK TIME: 53 minutes

3 eggs, separated	60 g apricot jam
170 g white chocolate, chopped	16 g icing sugar
120 g cream cheese, softened	14 g cocoa powder

1. Grease a 18 x 10 cm cake pan lightly.
2. Refrigerate the egg whites in a bowl to chill before using.
3. Microwave the chocolate and cream cheese on high for about 3 minutes.
4. Remove from the microwave and whisk in the egg yolks.
5. Whisk together egg whites until firm peaks form and combine with the chocolate mixture and cocoa powder. Transfer the mixture into the cake pan.
6. When ready to cook, remove the grill plate from basket 1 then preheat the airfryer basket for three minutes by activating the automatic preheat key.
7. Place the cake pan into basket 1 and set the temperature to 140°C for 30 minutes, then touch the start key to activate the airfryer.
8. When cooking is complete, dust the cheesecake with icing sugar and spread jam on top to serve.

Healthy Fruit Muffins

SERVES 6

| PREP TIME: 10 minutes
| COOK TIME: 10 minutes

240 ml semi-skimmed milk
1 pack Oreo biscuits, crushed
1 banana, peeled and chopped
1 apple, peeled, cored and chopped
4 g baking soda
4 g baking powder
5 ml honey
5 ml fresh lemon juice
2 g cocoa powder
Pinch of ground cinnamon

1. Grease 6 muffin cups lightly.
2. Mix the milk, biscuits, cocoa powder, baking soda and baking powder in a medium bowl until a smooth mixture is formed.
3. Divide this mixture evenly into the prepared muffin cups.
4. When ready to cook, remove the grill plates and preheat the airfryer baskets for three minutes by activating the automatic preheat key.
5. Place half of the muffin cups in a single layer in each basket. Select the Match Cook key then set basket 1 to 160°C for 10 minutes, then touch the start key to activate the airfryer. Bake until toothpick inserted in centre comes out clean.
6. When cooking is complete, transfer the muffin cups to a plate.
7. Mix the apple, banana, honey, lemon juice and cinnamon in a bowl.
8. Scoop out some portion from centre of muffins and fill with the fruit mixture. Refrigerate for 2 hours and serve chilled.

Bread Sultana Pudding

SERVES 2

| PREP TIME: 10 minutes
| COOK TIME: 12 minutes

240 ml milk
1 egg
2 bread slices, cut into small cubes
30 g sultanas, soaked in hot water for about 15 minutes
15 g chocolate chips
15 g sugar
12 g brown sugar
½ tsp. ground cinnamon
¼ tsp. vanilla extract

1. Grease a 18x13 cm baking dish lightly.
2. Mix the egg, milk, brown sugar, cinnamon and vanilla extract until well combined.
3. Stir in the sultanas and mix well.
4. Arrange the bread cubes evenly in the baking dish and pour in the milk mixture.
5. Refrigerate for about 20 minutes and sprinkle with chocolate chips and sugar.
6. When ready to cook, remove the grill plate from basket 1 then preheat the airfryer basket for three minutes by activating the automatic preheat key.
7. Place the baking dish into basket 1 and set the temperature to 190°C for 12 minutes, then touch the start key to activate the airfryer.
8. When cooking is complete, transfer the bread pudding to a plate. Serve hot.

Appendix 1: Tower Vortx Duo Basket Pre-Set Menu Table

The table below shows the pre-set times and cooking temperatures for each of the unit's 12 auto-cook menus.

PRE-SET FUNCTIONS	DEFAULT TIME	DEFAULT TEMP (°C)
PRE-HEAT	3 minsw	180°C
FRIES	18 mins	200°C
MEAT	12 mins	200°C
DRUMSTICKS	20 mins	200°C
STEAK	12 mins	180°C
CAKE	25 mins	160°C
PRAWN	8 mins	180°C
FISH	10 mins	180°C
PIZZA	20 mins	180°C
VEGETABLES	10 mins	160°C
RE-HEAT	15 mins	150°C
DEHYDRATE	6 hrs Adjustable time: 0.5 hr to 24 hrs	60°C

Appendix 2: Basic Kitchen Conversions & Equivalents

DRY MEASUREMENTS CONVERSION CHART

3 teaspoons = 1 tablespoon = 1/16 cup

6 teaspoons = 2 tablespoons = 1/8 cup

12 teaspoons = 4 tablespoons = ¼ cup

24 teaspoons = 8 tablespoons = ½ cup

36 teaspoons = 12 tablespoons = ¾ cup

48 teaspoons = 16 tablespoons = 1 cup

METRIC TO US COOKING

CONVERSIONS

OVEN TEMPERATURES

120 °C = 250 °F

160 °C = 320 °F

180 °C = 350 °F

205 °C = 400 °F

220 °C = 425 °F

LIQUID MEASUREMENTS

CONVERSION CHART

8 fluid ounces = 1 cup = ½ pint = ¼ quart

16 fluid ounces = 2 cups = 1 pint = ½ quart

32 fluid ounces = 4 cups = 2 pints = 1 quart = ¼
gallon

128 fluid ounces = 16 cups = 8 pints = 4

quarts = 1 gallon

BAKING IN GRAMS

1 cup flour = 140 grams

1 cup sugar = 150 grams

1 cup powdered sugar = 160 grams

1 cup heavy cream = 235 grams

VOLUME

1 milliliter = 1/5 teaspoon

5 ml = 1 teaspoon

15 ml = 1 tablespoon

240 ml = 1 cup or 8 fluid ounces

1 liter = 34 fluid ounces

WEIGHT

1 gram = .035 ounces

100 grams = 3.5 ounces

500 grams = 1.1 pounds

1 kilogram = 35 ounces

US TO METRIC COOKING CONVERSIONS

1/5 tsp = 1 ml

1 tsp = 5 ml

1 tbsp = 15 ml

1 fluid ounces = 30 ml

1 cup = 237 ml

1 pint (2 cups) = 473 ml

1 quart (4 cups) = .95 liter

1 gallon (16 cups) = 3.8 liters

1 oz = 28 grams

1 pound = 454 grams

BUTTER

1 cup butter = 2 sticks = 8 ounces = 230 grams = 16 tablespoons

WHAT DOES 1 CUP EQUAL

1 cup = 8 fluid ounces

1 cup = 16 tablespoons

1 cup = 48 teaspoons

1 cup = ½ pint

1 cup = ¼ quart

1 cup = 1/16 gallon

1 cup = 240 ml

BAKING PAN CONVERSIONS

9-inch round cake pan = 12 cups

10-inch tube pan =16 cups

10-inch bundt pan = 12 cups

9-inch springform pan = 10 cups

9 x 5 inch loaf pan = 8 cups

9-inch square pan = 8 cups

BAKING PAN CONVERSIONS

1 cup all-purpose flour = 4.5 oz

1 cup rolled oats = 3 oz

1 large egg = 1.7 oz

1 cup butter = 8 oz

1 cup milk = 8 oz

1 cup heavy cream = 8.4 oz

1 cup granulated sugar = 7.1 oz

1 cup packed brown sugar = 7.75 oz

1 cup vegetable oil = 7.7 oz

1 cup unsifted powdered sugar = 4.4 oz

Appendix 3: Recipes Index

Printed in Great Britain
by Amazon

36398292R00044